A Mother's Dream

Unbeatable Ajji and
her unforgettable flavours

Nayana Shreekant Mallapurkar

Published by

Office : D-328, Defence Colony, New Delhi-110024
Mobiles: +91-9810539784, +91-9833283155
Emails: ganivpanjrath@yahoo.co.in, tannaazirani@gmail.com

Copyright © 2021 Nayana Shreekant Mallapurkar
Illustrations credits: Zeba Rizvi

Disclaimer

No part of the book may be reproduced, stored in a retrieval system, or transmitted in any form by any means, electronic, mechanical, photocopying, recording or otherwise, without the prior written permission from the publishers.

The views, content and opinion expressed in the book are the individual assertion and opinion of the author and the publisher does not take any responsibility for the same in any manner whatsoever. The same shall solely be the responsibility of the author.

ISBN-13: 978-81-949782-3-7
ISBN 10: 81-949782-3-8

MRP: $15

Printed at Thomson Press, New Delhi

Dedicated to my Maama Shri Sadanand Hosalkar, my Aunts Mrs. Radha Nayak and Dr. Sushila Kerkar and my Mother Mrs. Sunita Mallapurkar

The legacy continues....

PREFACE

This book is dedicated to my Ajji and my Uncle, my two Aunts and Mother. In writing this book I am paying my tribute to my Ajji (my maternal Grandmother), to her strength, determination and zeal for life. It is through her that we (both my brothers and myself) are blessed to have our Mother who has been our pillar of strength. With her 'Never say die' attitude and persistent perseverance my Mother has been a role model for us to live our lives differently.

A sincere thank you to all those family members, friends and well-wishers for extending their support to my Ajji that has contributed and enabled her to sail through this journey of life.

This book is also dedicated to all those individuals out there who are facing life's challenges and going through their weak moments in life to not give up. Stay focused and have faith because all will be well!

Best wishes always
Nayana Shreekant Mallapurkar

THANK YOU NOTE

This book has been my Mother's dream. I have grown up listening to all the stories mentioned in this book and it was her desire that a book be written on her Mother. It is for her that I took up this beautiful task and I must say it has been a very satisfying and serene feeling to have been able to fulfill her dream. So, thank you Amma (Mother) for sharing the stories and sowing the seed for writing this book.

I would like to extend my gratitude to my Maama and Maami(Sadanand and Shobha Hosalkar) for sharing their experiences that has contributed to this book.

I would like to acknowledge my friend Reshma Pai for her creative thoughts and inputs that has helped in shaping this book. My friend and mentor Nirmala S for her support and encouragement. The first draft of the book was shared with Reshma and Nirmala. Their suggestions and critical analysis have been encouraging and kept me motivated.

Special thanks to Jacintha Saldanha, my school teacher. Our relationship has grown from a teacher student relation to being great friends. Thank you for all the love and support. And special thanks for extending your assistance with the proof reading.

A big thank you to my editor and publishers at Creative Crows Publishers LLP, Tannaaz Irani and Ganiv Chadha Panjrath for ensuring my thoughts were constructively expressed. Thank you to Zeba Rizvi for the lovely illustrations and patiently accommodating my inputs. Special thanks to Mosiur Rehman for the beautiful cover page design. You caught my thoughts bang on!

This is my first book, and I was very apprehensive about how it was going to shape up. However, the encouraging feedback from Reshma, Nirmala, Jacintha, Tannaaz, my brothers Sachin and Ajay, Preeti(my sister-in-law), Archana Joshi and Anuprita Arora (my friends) have awakened the writer in me. Thank you very much for all the kind words!

CONTENTS

Prologue	10-14
1. The Beginning of a Journey	15-17
2. The Storm	18-22
3. Moving On	23-38
4. A New Chapter	39-70
5. Some New Relationships	71-118

Notes:
a.	List of Recipes	119
b.	General Cooking Tips	120-121

PROLOGUE

DON'T QUIT

When things go wrong, as they sometimes will,
When the road you're trudging seems all uphill,
When funds are low and the debts are high,
And you want to smile but you have to sigh,
When care is pressing you down a bit,
Rest if you must, but don't you quit.
Life is queer with its twists and turns,
As every one of us sometimes learns,
And many a failure turns about,
When he might have won if he'd stuck it out.
Don't give up, though the pace seems slow -
You may succeed with another blow.
Often the goal is nearer than
It seems to a faint and faltering man;
Often the struggler has given up
When he might have captured the victor's cup,
And he learned too late, when the night slipped down,
How close he was to the golden crown.
Success is failure turned inside out -
The silver tint of the clouds of doubt,
And you never can tell how close you are -
It may be near when it seems afar;
So stick to the fight when you're hardest hit -
It's when things seem worst that you mustn't quit.

- by John Greenleaf Whittier

I have been toying with the idea of writing a book for the past eight to nine years. Today on the 9th of September, 2018 I finally decided to get started. I had been wondering in agony about how I must begin writing. And as luck would have it, I happened to get sight of Mr. Pillai's book titled 'How to Write a Book'. This book has, in many ways, inspired me to get my thoughts together and start writing.

My book is based on Smt. Sitabai R Hoslakar (Ajji), my maternal Grandmother, "Ajji", that is what we addressed her as. I have been fortunate enough to be in the company of my Grandmother until my teen years. The experience of having grandparents around in many ways contributes to the development and the shaping of values in the life of a grandchild. In any normal circumstance, at any given time, there are three generations interacting and residing in society. So, in a way, the possibility for exchange of values and learning and carrying forward the legacy can be transited to the next generation smoothly. As a child, I have always heard stories from my Mother and her siblings – of their harsh and stressful childhood journeys, and how my Ajji as a single Mother sailed through the difficult times with her grit and courage. I have witnessed occasions when my Mother with my Maama (maternal uncle) and Pachis (maternal aunts) would be fondly recalling their childhood memories of their Mother and would either have a hearty laugh or feel solemn about the past unpleasant experiences. However, most of the time they would be all praises for their Mother's determination and foresightedness. I have never once heard my Mother and her siblings ever mention anything unworthy about her personality and character. They have always been in awe of her persona. It's been more than thirty years since her demise, but her memories stand very strong and they narrate the same stories with the same depth and fondness amongst themselves and with others. Such is the strength of the beautiful bond between the Mother and her children.

During the early years of my life, I would take keen interest in extending a helping hand in the kitchen to my Mother. Most of my cooking skills have been acquired from my Mother. And she had acquired it from her Mother. She would narrate her childhood memories while cooking some of the traditional recipes. All these narratives have made a profound impact on me as a daughter and I felt it was only apt for me to pen it down; both my Ajji's life journey as well as her mouthwatering delicacies, in the hope of keeping it alive for the generations to follow. Her life's journey will remind us of our roots and the aspirations and struggles of this one Lady who set the ball rolling for her future generations. While the recipes of the traditional delicacies will keep us anchored to our native taste buds, as opposed to the synthetic taste buds of today's culinary lifestyle.

Her life is a message to all of us. It is because of her that we enjoy the advancement and pleasures of life. It is because of her that each upcoming generation continues to build on the legacy in an incremental manner only to rise to an even higher level. The legacy referred to is not in terms of worldly accomplishment, but in terms of the in-born character of courage, grit, perseverance, hope and faith. It will be a reminder for us in times of our weak moments, in times when we feel we don't have the strength to go on, in times when we see no hope – to remember to have faith in ourselves and the Creator. And in doing so continue to move on, because you have a dream and you know it will manifest and all will be well.

"You have to dream before your dreams can come true."
- A. P. J. Abdul Kalam

There are those who dream by night and there are those who dream by the day. The only difference between the two is that those who dream by the day take the courage to act out their dreams in reality to make it possible and 'live the dream'.

It is said, "Whatever you do, or dream you can, begin it. Boldness has genius and power and magic in it."
- Johann Wolfgang von Goethe.

We all have grown up listening and reading inspirational stories of successful people – be they of sports personalities, actors, businessmen, political leaders, bankers, investors, scientists, social activists or writers, who fought against all odds; their perseverance, their dreams and visions, their setbacks and how they maneuvered through all hardships to achieve their goals and dreams.

We have examples of the likes of Mahatma Gandhi who dreamt of an Independent India. Jamsetji Tata who built the first Taj Hotel in the pre-independence era as a fitting reply to the British arrogance, Nelson Mandela for his dream of a free South Africa, Sir Edmund Percival Hillary, Sherpa mountaineer Tenzing Norgay who became the first climbers confirmed to have reached the summit of Mount Everest, the inventions of Albert Einstein and Alexander Graham Bell that changed the world, to the most recent Tim Berners-Lee who gave us the world wide web and the wonders that followed with it.

"Dreams come true. Without that possibility, nature would not incite us to have them."

– John Updike

Most of my Ajji's life experiences have been shared with me by my Mother, who refers to my Grandmother as a "Super Star" and has been her "Biggest Fan" from the time she grew up. My Mother always narrates, that it was Ajji's dream to ensure that she provides the best for her children. She wanted to ensure that the many lives that she had brought into the world, were protected and nurtured to live the life they were meant for. Through this book I have made an attempt to recount her efforts and courage to walk the path and make her dream come true.

"We all have dreams. But in order to make dreams come into reality, it takes an awful lot of determination, dedication, self-discipline, and effort"

- *Jesse Owens*

1

The Beginning Of A Journey

"All of life is peaks and valleys. Don't let the peaks get too high and the valleys too low."

-John Wooden

Ajji, was born as Ms. Gulab Bai Kumtha around the year 1920 in Sirsi, a small village in Kumta, North Canara (Karnataka, India). At that point of time, Sirsi was a very small village with very limited basic amenities. The place is surrounded by forests, and the region has a number of waterfalls. However, today, Sirsi is a flourishing town and is the largest city and a business hub in North Canara district. It is known for the 16th century Marikamba Temple dedicated to a form of the goddess Durga. The region is also known for spices such as cardamom, pepper, betel leaves, and vanilla.

Ajji was the only child to her parents. She lost her mother when she was five months old. And I am given to understand that she lost her father as well during those tender growing years. She was raised by her maternal grandmother. In terms of education, she attended school till grade VI, and in keeping with social norms prevalent then, where the role of most women was limited to being the homemaker, she fell in line too. A suitable alliance was found and she moved on to pursue her journey of being a homemaker and raising a family, as was expected. Ajji entered the state of wedlock in her early teen years, at about sixteen years of age.

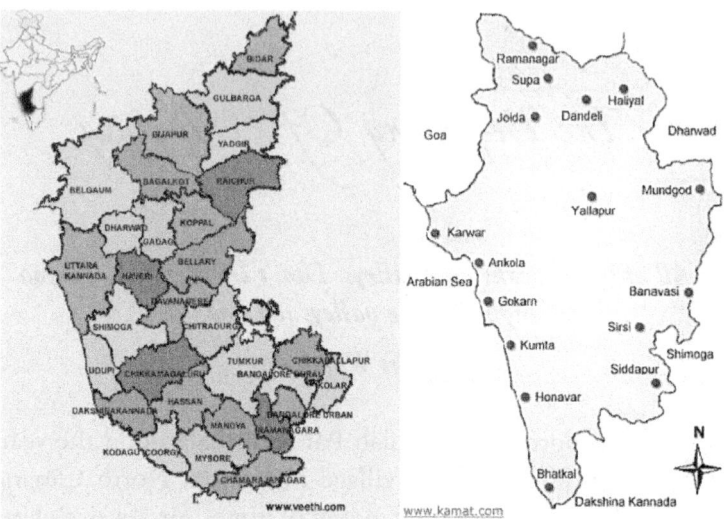

www.veethi.com & www.kamat.com
Note: *North Canara is also referred as Uttara Kannada*

Not much can be recalled about my Grandfather, Ramachandra as he was known. From whatever I gather, I imagine him to be five feet and eight inches tall, a moderately built individual with a wheatish complexion. It is learnt that he had lost his father at a very young age. He and my great grandmother were part of a joint family and hence continued to be part of his paternal family. Overall, the family had a modest background. It is believed he was a man of principles. He was very disciplined and enjoyed a lot of respect from family members and others. My Mother recalls that distant relatives have memories of my grandfather that expressed great appreciation for him and the values he lived by. He was known for his sincerity and his genuine nature.

The Beginning Of A Journey

My Grandfather worked in the Civil Services. He was employed as an overseer in the Public Works Department (PWD). His job required him to be transferred quite often, and hence the family had to relocate several times. They led a decent lifestyle and had acquired a reasonable amount of wealth. Life was good and they were blessed with three children (one son and two daughters) and awaiting the arrival of the fourth child. During this time, they were staying in a place called Siddapur, North Canara. He was deputed on the Gerusoppaa Falls Dam project.

Today Siddapur is considered as a hill station town. Gerusoppaa Falls or Joga Jalapatha and Jogada Gundi as known in the regional Kannada language is famously known as the Jog Falls. It is the second highest plunge waterfall in India as it drops directly and does not stream on to the rocks. Associated with the waterfall is the nearby Linganmakki Dam across the river Sharavathi, and the Hydro-Electric Power Station that it serves. The Power Station has been operational since 1949, and is, at 1200 MW capacity, one of the largest Hydro-Electric Power stations in India and a significant source of electric power for Karnataka.

"However difficult life may seem, there is always something you can do and succeed at."
                                                                             -*Stephen Hawking*

2

The Storm

> *"Sometimes life hits you in the head with a brick. Don't lose faith"*
> *-Steve Jobs*

Life then was a normal routine, with my Grandfather occupied in his job and my Grandmother busy with the regular household chores and motherhood responsibilities. They were blessed with three children and expecting the birth of their fourth child, my Mother. My Maama being the eldest was four years old and my two Pachis - Radha Pachi two years old and Sushil Pachi was ten months old. It was the year 1942, when one fine day all hell broke loose. My Grandfather unexpectedly succumbed to his death. The reasons are unknown. He was only twenty-eight years of age.

I cannot even begin to imagine how devastated my Ajji must have been at that time. Though the movement was inevitable, for a young widow (aged twenty-two) with three children and bearing a child in her womb, I am sure my Maama and Pachis were not even able to fathom the gravity of the situation at that tender age. It must have been worse than being struck by a thunderbolt. I am certain she must have been in a state of shock, not knowing how to respond to what was changing around her.

The Storm

I sometimes marvel at her emotional state at that tender age, enveloped by uncertainty. What thoughts must have run through her mind? She might have asked herself 'Why me?' 'Where do I go now?' 'How do I take care of my kids?' 'Do I have an option of getting rid of my unborn child?' 'Should I just end it all?'- and many more.

It must have given her sleepless nights. I am sure, Ajji must have been hounded by all these questions and challenges that life had thrown her way. I am very certain that Ajji never slept peacefully for many nights from that day on, for many years to come.

She lived in an era, where a woman's identity was linked either to her father's or husband's name. In the absence of both, she was, in many ways sidelined almost as if she did not exist. Our laws relating to inheritance were also weak, in that, they were unfavourable to women and that made things more difficult.

The saying, that 'those who stand by you in your weakest moments are your true friends' was put to test. With the death of my Grandfather, Ajji was set adrift with no anchor in sight. Her in-laws refused to extend any support. All turned a blind eye to the fact that she was due to deliver her fourth child. She was not permitted to return to the family house. From the maternal side too, she had lost all her support. Her grandmother who had raised her had also passed away. As she was the only child of her parents, the maternal family included the extended family only. It is said that when all doors are closed, God somewhere opens a window. One of Ajji's maternal uncles from the extended family, stood strong by her side in those difficult times. When he realised her difficult position, he immediately rushed to her rescue and brought her back with him to Kumta and provided her shelter in his house.

Ajji's uncle was supposedly a rich and kind man. However, I am given to understand that the others in the household were not very appreciative of his action. And hence, the rest of the household was reluctant in accepting them. Thus, the support extended by the rest of the household was not out of love and care, but rather, on humanitarian grounds. In a sense, it was a major obligation as suddenly there were five extra mouths to feed; a burden even for a wealthy home.

My Mother was born at this time. The arrival of my Mother in these circumstances surely did not invite celebrations. In fact, nobody even recorded the date of birth. So, amongst all her siblings, my Mother is the only one who does not celebrate her birthday. Rather, she is very uncomfortable to even make a mention of it. Even we, as her children, are not allowed to celebrate it.

Every single day brought a keen torture to Ajji. Every single day she would be reminded by the lady of the house what a nuisance and pain this family of five had been and how their presence was impacting their family life and lifestyle. Ajji I am sure, tolerated the humiliation considering the vulnerability of the situation. She had no option but to silently and patiently bear the unpleasantly vitiated atmosphere in order to protect the new born child and the other kids, and ensure a shelter for all of them. So, she continued to accept the support extended, albeit with a heavy heart. I guess she continued like this for close to a year. At one point when she could not handle it anymore, or rather was pushed so much to the edge that she decided to move out of the house.

The Storm

What A Pain...She Is An Absolute Nuisance

The harsh treatment meted out to her during those difficult years made it difficult to heal the wound of her loss and left a huge scar on Ajji's heart. Filled with rage, hurt and sheer helplessness at the treatment that was meted out to her, by these people, she decided to cut off all ties with this family. I am told by my Mother, that Ajji was very bitter within her heart, about the treatment she got from her family over a period of time. She had always been very reluctant to narrate any memories of the past. She just chose to not speak much about them. Maybe, it brought back to life her worst nightmarish reality from the dead past.

The decision to cut ties with the family, was one that she regretted later in her life. My Mother would always make a mention of this regret. So, on one occasion, I asked my

A Mother's Dream

Mother what this regret was about. My Mother explained to me that the circumstances of Ajji's early life were something she was unprepared for. The economic situation during those times was not that great for anyone. Given her education level and general exposure to life, she was so overwhelmed that she probably was unrealistic and immature in her expectations from others. Upon introspection on yesteryear, she realised that she herself was in a state of denial of the realities of life, and probably harbored a victim mentality that made her view life differently. Hence, in those circumstances, she was furious with her interpretation of others' behaviour and when reason was overcome by fury, made a decision to cut ties. However, having matured and evolved with life experiences she was now able to sympathize with the reluctance exhibited by the other household members. She appreciated the support from her uncle in those times. She realised that both conjugal and consanguineous families play a very important role in one's life; and that it was important to maintain and nurture these ties vis-à-vis socialization and kinship. My Mother recalls, that as a result of these circumstances, they never had the opportunity to engage with members of their extended family. My Mother does not have any childhood memories of interacting with or knowing any of her cousins. They remained a tightly knit nuclear family, till of course, they grew up and got married. In narrating this my Mother passed on a very important life-lesson to me that she got from Ajji; and that is to never ever break ties with your family.

"The only rock I know that stays steady, the only institution I know that works, is the family."

-Lee Iacocca

3

Moving On

"Life is a series of natural and spontaneous changes. Don't resist them - that only creates sorrow. Let reality be reality. Let things flow naturally forward in whatever way they like."

-Lao Tzu

In the neighborhood lived Rukmini Bai - Bai in English means woman. A bond had developed between her and Ajji. Rukmini Bai had some spare rooms at her house. My Maama recalls that they eventually moved into her house, which Rukmini Bai rented out to Ajji. According to my Maama, Rukmini Bai had a soft corner for my Ajji and he was not sure if she ever collected the rent from my Ajji. And thus, began the new phase of my Ajji's life. She needed to support her family. With no specific education or skills to take up employment, she would support the family with what she earned by doing all sorts of odd jobs. In the initial days it included extending her services as a household help. So, during the day time she was occupied with household work in the neighborhood and would be occupied with completing tailoring jobs in the late night hours. She was good at embroidery, knitting and other kinds of handicraft. All these skills were self-learnt. She somehow was gifted at this. Apparently, my Ajji was good at stitching ladies' and children's apparel. I can vouch for this too, as I have personally witnessed some of her creations. In the latter days of her life, her favourite pastime was knitting. She would knit beautiful sweaters for new born babies. She would make a complete set, which included a sweater, a head cap and cute tiny little socks. My Mother has still retained one set in her remembrance.

My Mother always narrates, that though they did not have any close family, they were always blessed to have a treasure trove of well-wishers who extended timely support. Some of them were far off relatives or neighbours or mere acquaintances. This led to establishing new ties and bonds that were very strong and continue to last till date.

One such bond was with Ajji's maternal Uncle, fondly referred to as Ram Maama. He lived in a nearby district and was aware of Ajji's hardships. He was engaged in Government service as a postman earning a salary of six or seven rupees per month. My Maama tells me that Ram Maama would send a money order of two rupees every month to my Ajji as financial support till the time my Ajji got a job.

It is quite amazing and nearly impossible to even relate to the one-digit salary figures in comparison to the five digit and above salary figures of today. Though I have never met this Maama, I can surely say, that he was a large-hearted soul. Two rupees amounted to almost 33% of his salary, which he willingly contributed to help my Ajji make ends meet; not just for a month or two, but for a long period of four to five years. He was a caring and affectionate uncle. Every time he visited Kumta, he would choose to stay at Ajji's residence and spend quality time with the children. My Mother tells me that Ram Maama had his extended family living in Kumta, but he would only visit them; his base station would always be their home. Ajji had a lot of love and gratitude for this Maama.

While I write this, I take this as an opportunity to thank him and his family for all their support extended to Ajji. I can imagine the adjustments the lady of the house would have had to make with a 33% cut in her household income for a period of four to five years, which went a long way in stabilizing my Ajji in those times.

During this period, I am sure Ajji was walking on a tight rope. Though there were hardships, she also recalls the support that was extended to her especially by her neighbours, by way of caring for her children while she was out at work or extending support when the kids needed medical attention and being there with her. I once asked my Maama, if he recalled what life was like in those times. He stated his memories were not pleasant and were more to do with the struggle he had to face as there was not much support from immediate family members, money was a concern and food was a major scarcity.

He recalls that in the years 1944-45 during World War II there was a major shortage of food. Some parts of the country faced famine, especially Bengal. It was around this time that the Government of India introduced the Public Distribution System. This was a food security system established by the Government to distribute food and non-food items at subsidized rates. Major commodities distributed included staple food grains, such as wheat, rice, sugar and essential fuels like kerosene, through a network of fair price shops (also known as ration shops). To buy these items one needed to have a ration card. The items from these shops were much cheaper but were of average quality. My Maama recalls that during that time, due to shortage of food, rice in particular was not available in the ration shops. So, rice, which was a staple food, had to be procured from outside. Due to the scarcity of food, the Government was also very vigilant and

A Mother's Dream

kept a watch on any malpractices. Maama narrated that he and Ajji had to go to the neighbouring village, Manaki to purchase rice. Obviously, there were no privileges of having your own transportation or the ability to use public transportation. So, they had to walk all the way to Manaki, a distance of about four to five kilometers. Maama, was like the strong pillar of the household right from childhood. He had to shoulder the responsibilities along with Ajji. He recalls, how he would be actively involved in all activities with Ajji. He recalls their visit to Manaki to buy rice. After the purchase of the rice apparently, they would make two bundles, a small bundle for Maama and a big one for herself and carry it back home on their head.

Maama mentioned it was very ironic, there were times when they had the groceries but had no money to buy wood or vice versa. In those times, most household kitchens would operate on small earthen or brick stoves 'Chulha' that used wood as fuel. During such time my Ajji and Maama would visit the local saw mills and collect the unused or unusable wood lying around.

He recalls two distinct dishes, that were regular preparations in the household in those times. One was a porridge made from the millet called Finger Millet or Nachni also known as Ragi. The porridge would be made of the flour and was called "Ambil". The other dish was a rice pancake called 'Mumri (thalipeeth)'. However, today Nachni is widely used as a dietary supplement for its nutritional values. It is rich in fiber, and therefore good for weight watchers. Apart from this, it helps in controlling blood sugar levels, reduces cholesterol, makes excellent food for toddlers. The nachni porridge was known as a poor man's meal because about three to four tablespoons spoons of nachni flour would provide for a one-time meal for the family. This would occasionally be served with a side dish of fish fry or some curry or curds.

A Mother's Dream

Recipe No 1: Aambil
(Serves 2)

Ingredients
- 2-3 tbsp Nachni* flour
- 4 glasses of water (one L)
- Salt

To serve with (any one of the below)
- Curds
- Fish curry
- Vegetable curry

Preparation
1) Soak nachni flour in one glass of water (250 mL) for one hour.
2) Mix the soaked nachni with the remaining three glasses of water in a cooking pot and keep on slow flame to cook.
3) Keep stirring to avoid formation of lumps.
4) Once the mixture starts boiling, stir till it gets to a semi liquid consistency.
5) Add salt to taste.
6) Serve with Curds / fish curry / vegetable curry.

Optional
Add 1 tbsp of cooked granular rice "Kanik" or cooked rice to the Aambil. This will make the meal filling.

Note
*Also known as Ragi or Finger Millet.

The other regular dish was the Mumri. This is my all-time favourite dish. I ensure I have this at least once a week for breakfast. It's a delicious breakfast item and goes very well with homemade white butter.

My Mother recalls, Ajji would make one big 'Mumri' on a large tava. Then make four pieces of it. A slightly bigger piece for Maama (as he had a better appetite than the others) and 3 pieces for the daughters. She would not eat anything herself. That was a main dish for the household. She would grind the rice to a coarse flour on the 'Jatha' at home. Jatha is a stone grinder operated manually.

Recipe No 2: Mumri (Thalipeeth)
(Serves 2)

Ingredients
- 1 cup (125 gms) of rava rice (optional rice flour is also fine)
- 1 medium sized onion finely chopped
- 1 green chilli finely chopped
- 2.5 cm / 1 inch fresh ginger finely chopped / grated
- 2 tbsp finely chopped coriander leaves
- 3 tbsp fresh grated coconut
- Salt
- 1 ½ glass of water (to add as per consistency required)
- Oil

To serve with (Any one of the below)
- Homemade white butter
- Salted butter
- Coconut chutney

Preparation
1) In a bowl add the rava rice and add 1 glass water and let the rava rice soak in it. Let it rest for 10-15 minutes (you will notice that all the water has got absorbed in the rava rice).
2) Add all the ingredients except oil to the soaked rice.
3) Add water to make a semi-thick batter.
4) Heat a flat pan. Smear oil and spread the batter on the pan like a pancake.
5) Cover the pan and let it cook on the steam it generates.
6) Pour some oil on the sides of the pan cake and turn it on the other side.
7) Serve with homemade white butter.

Another memory my Maama shared was about the Poha (Beaten rice) making mill in the neighbourhood. Apparently, the good quality Poha would be separated and the rest of the residue which was not saleable would be kept separately and would be sold at a very low price by the owner in the neighborhood. Ajji would regularly procure this item from the mill owner. Known for her cooking skills she would produce an amazing variety of dishes, each having a unique taste. This would break the monotony for her children. Two of these Poha dishes that we still continue to relish are, one that I call Instant Poha and the other Sweet Poha.

Recipe No 3: Poha (Beaten Rice)
(Serves 2)

Ingredients
- 2 cups (250gm) thin beaten rice (poha)
- 1 medium sized onion finely chopped
- 1 dry red chilli (Byadgi) roasted
- 1 tsp jaggery
- 1 tbsp water
- 1 cup fresh grated coconut
- Salt
- 1 tbsp coriander leaves chopped

To serve with
- 50 gm Sev

Preparation
1) In a bowl crush the roasted red chilli (like flakes).
2) Add jaggery, water and mix.
3) Add the finely chopped onion, fresh grated coconut, thin beaten rice and salt.
4) Crush all together and mix well.
5) Garnish with coriander leaves and sev.

Recipe No 4: Sweet Poha
(With Banana and Coconut Milk)
Traditionally called Hashaal
(Serves 2)

Ingredients
- 2 cups (200 gm) thick beaten rice (Poha)
- 1 medium banana cut into small pieces
- 1 glass (250 mL) of coconut milk
- Jaggery as per taste
- ½ tsp of green cardamom (Elaichi) powder
- 1 glass (250 mL) water
- Salt (1 pinch)

Preparation
1) Soak the thick beaten rice in water and strain immediately.
2) In a bowl add the coconut milk and dissolve the jaggery into it.
3) Add the banana pieces and soaked beaten rice and garnish with the cardamom powder and salt.

Variation
Banana can be replaced with 1 cup of muskmelon (cut into small pieces).

Cooking Tip
This dish should be prepared just 15-20 minutes before you are ready to consume it to maintain the texture of the ingredients. Otherwise, it gets soggy.

Recipe No 5: Idli Chura
(Serves 2)

Ingredients
- 5 - 6 leftover idli crumbled
- 1 medium sized onion finely chopped
- 1 green chili finely chopped
- 2 tbsp fresh grated coconut
- Salt
- ½ tsp of sugar
- 1 tbsp chopped coriander leaves
- 1 tsp pure coconut oil (optional)

Preparation
1) Place the crumbled idli in a bowl.
2) Add the finely chopped onion, green chillies, fresh grated coconut, sugar, salt and pure coconut oil and mix well.
3) Garnish with coriander leaves.

This is another regular dish churned from the leftovers of Idli was the Idli Chura. And if the budgets permitted, some of the slightly elite breakfast dishes they would be fortunate to relish were red pumpkin Dhodak (dhokla) or Dosa.

Recipe No 6: Red pumpkin Dhodak (dhokla)
(Serves: 2)

Ingredients
- 1 cup rice rava or semolina
- 250 gm red pumpkin (grated)
- ½ cup fresh grated coconut
- Jaggery as per taste
- 1 tsp green cardamom (Elaichi) powder
- 1 pinch of salt
- 1 tsp ghee
- ½ cup water

To serve with
- Ghee

Preparation
1) Mix all the ingredients to make a semi thick batter.
2) Take a flat-bottomed vessel and coat with ghee and pour the mixture in the vessel.
3) Steam in pressure cooker without the whistle till done or in a steamer.
4) Cut in pieces and serve hot with ghee.

Variation
- One has the option of making it much richer by adding cashew nuts and a bit of grated coconut to the mix.
- Another variation was to mix the ingredients to give it a consistency of pancake batter and make pancakes of the same.
- Instead of red pumpkin, one also has the option to add grated white pumpkin, cucumber or watermelon rind.

A Mother's Dream

It took my Ajji close to five years (1942 to 1947) to stabilize herself from the loss and to get a grip on life, to be able to start thinking about the way forward. She was blessed to be surrounded by well-wishers, who were witnessing her struggle and courage given the harsh realities of life. These well-wishers had now started extending their generous support to help her move forward. Having experienced the dark realities of life she had vowed to herself that her children would never ever face the same hardships. Her only dream since then was to ensure that she made her children financially and emotionally strong individuals. And so, the journey began. Being educated only till class VI she had to make the best out of the opportunities available to her. It was important to acquire skills that would make her employable immediately.

Some amount of brainstorming with well-wishers, helped narrow down options and it was decided that she pursue a one-year course in nursing. This course would also provide for some stipend, which would help her to sustain body and mind. The closest Nursing Institute happened to be in Karwar. It was decided that she would move to Karwar and pursue the course. Moving to Karwar was all very well, but the next concern was how would she sustain herself for a year in Karwar, along with four children aged nine years, seven years, five years and four years respectively. It was not possible to move with all the children to Karwar. While she would enroll in the nursing course it was equally important to work towards nurturing the growth and educational requirement of the children in a safe and conducive environment.

It is said that when you truly wish for something, the universal forces come together to make it a reality. A few good God sent guardians came forward to make this happen. Among the well-wishers were a prominent lawyer Mr. Mahimkurve, a Local School teacher Mr. Dhareshwar and one Mr. Hegde. Together they managed to get things sorted. Mr. Hegde accepted the responsibility to support my Maama (the eldest of the lot) for the one-year period with his schooling and boarding requirement. Mr. Mahimkurve, through his connections arranged for the schooling and boarding of both my aunts at the famous shelter Maharshi Karve Stree Shikshan Samstha, (MKSSS), Pune. And the youngest daughter, my Mother, being too young was supposed to continue living with Ajji. It must have been a very hard decision to have your children part from you at an age when they needed parental warmth and care, but that seemed to be the most appropriate decision at the time.

My Mother recalls Ajji's anxiety and helplessness during those times. My Ajji was deeply haunted by the thought that because of her inability to provide for her children, her children had to be separated from her at a tender age. She consented to this arrangement with a heavy heart. I am sure this experience has made a deep impact on each of the family members; and the experiences during this phase have shaped their character for the good.

"Out of suffering have emerged the strongest souls; the most massive characters are seared with scars."

-Khalil Gibran

4

A New Chapter

"Nothing in life is to be feared, it is only to be understood. Now is the time to understand more, so that we may fear less."
-Marie Curie

Ajji continued to move forward and the days ahead painted a new hope. I am sure the beginning must have been a mixed bag of emotions. She had to embrace a new way of life. The journey she now undertook was seemingly into an immense void, an uncertainty and yet comforting. This was the first step towards her dream on which she walked with faith. The dream had its share of good and not so good memories. It brought in relationships that were cherished for the rest of her life.

So, the enrolment for the nursing programme was done and with the help of well-wishers she rented out a small room for herself and my Mother. My Mother at that time was about four years old. Apparently, the landlady and the neighboring families were very helpful and volunteered to be caretakers and babysitters for my Mother, while Ajji attended the nursing course. For the next twelve months, my Mother basked in the loving care and attention of these lovely families, while my Ajji successfully strived to complete her course. One such family next door, was that of Mr. Gopinath Bandekar. Gopinath Maama treated Ajji like a sister. He and his wife (Maami) along with their seven children became our extended family. They would ensure that my Mother was well fed and cared for. Most of the Bandekar family members are now settled in Mumbai and are part of the one another's family celebrations. On one such occasion, I have witnessed the Bandekars recalling childhood days and how, when my Mother would get naughty and difficult to control, they would pinch her. They all burst into laughter recalling all the childhood pranks they would play on her. My Mother has faint childhood memories of some of these lovely people. However, the relationship with this family has been strong. We are still connected to the members of this family and share a sweet bond. With them around, the completion of the nursing training was indeed like a dream for my Ajji.

During this period, my Maama sort of settled down with Mr. Hegde in Kumta. Maama would help Hegde Maama in his shop in his free time, While Radha and Sushil Pachi, tried to get their bearings at the Karve Institute in Pune. I am sure this one year had been difficult for all of them, with not much contact with one another and the uncertainty of what the future had to unfold.

Ajji successfully completed the nursing course. Her first posting was in a government hospital in Yellapur. Very soon, she moved to Yellapur, where she spent most of her life before moving to Mumbai. In those times Yellapur was a small village. Today it is recognized as a proper town. I have been visiting Yellapur regularly from my childhood and I see the change in the place over the years. All the villages and towns of North Canara are situated amidst thick forests and house some famous waterfalls. Yellapur holds as a tourist attraction today. It is famously known for the Sathodi Falls and Magod Falls among others. It is also known for the Siddhis of

Karnataka. The Siddhis are an ethnic group inhabiting India. Members, the descendants of the Bantu people from Southeast Africa, that were brought to the Indian subcontinent as slaves by the Portuguese merchants. There is a Siddhi population fifty thousand strong across India, of which more than a third live in Karnataka. I remember once, when I was in Yellapur and noticed them in the marketplace and as a child was curious to know what these Africans were doing in that small town. That's when my Mother enlightened me with these facts. They really stand out in a group. Every time I visit Yellapur, I get a chance to see them and it is amazing to realize the unique African features that they still retain. I guess they conduct themselves in a very close community bond leaving very little scope for polarization.

 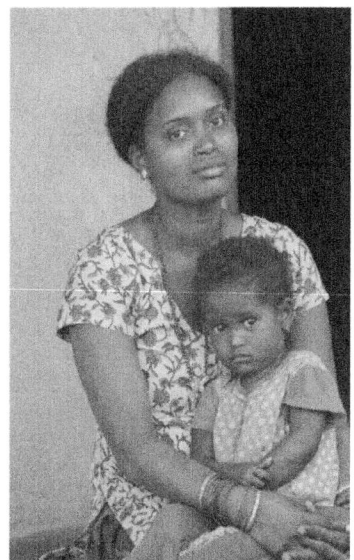

Photo Credit: https://www.beontheroad.com

At Yellapur, Ajji rented a small house close to her place of work. My Mother recalls a funny story related to the rented house. It seems that the landlords were pure vegetarian and had let out the house assuming my Ajji was a vegetarian too.

A Mother's Dream

In those times the staple food was steamed rice and fish curry. So, in the event of the landlord visiting them during meal time, they would ensure that the lunch plate that had fish served was covered with the steamed rice to camouflage the fish in the plate. According to my Mother, my Ajji's recipe of fish curry was outstanding. Even after so many years, it is said that the curry she cooked could not be mastered by any of the siblings. The recipe as my Mother learned from her Mother is mentioned here.

A New Chapter

Recipe No 7: Fish Curry
(Serves 2)

Ingredients
- 4 fish fillets (Pomfret, King fish, Rawas, Black pomfret)
- 1 cup fresh grated coconut
- 1 small onion finely chopped
- ½ small tomato finely chopped
- A leaflet of curry leaves
- 6 roasted garlic cloves
- Coriander leaves finely chopped
- 2 tbsp pure coconut oil or any regular cooking oil
- ½ tsp of rice soaked in 1 tbsp water
- 5 kokum petals
- Salt
- Water

Main Masala (Roast on pan and finely grind to powder)
- 4 dry red chillies (Byadgi)*
- 1 tbsp coriander seeds
- ½ tsp cumin seeds
- ¼ tsp fenugreek (methi) seeds

To serve with
- Steamed rice

Preparation
1) Heat the pure coconut oil in a pan. Add the onions, tomatoes, curry leaves and stir till light brown.
2) Grind to a smooth paste the grated coconut, main masala, roasted garlic and the soaked rice.
3) Add this paste to the onions and stir with some water to get semi thick consistency.

4) Add the fish fillets, salt to taste and the kokum petals and bring to boil and simmer for ten minutes.
5) Garnish with chopped coriander leaves.
6) Serve with steamed rice.

Note
*Byadgi chilli is a famous variety of chilli mainly grown in Karnataka. It is known for its deep red colour and is less spicy.

Cooking tip
Soaked rice when added while grinding works as a thickening ingredient.

The recipe for fish curry is a standard recipe; this was followed with some variations if cooked with prawns or mussels. One more finger licking variation is with dry prawns and raw papaya (cut into small pieces). This variation goes best with the parboiled rice, traditionally called 'peise' (Congi). During the mango season, Ajji would add a few pieces of raw mango and drum sticks to the prawn and mussel curry. The raw mango and drumstick would give the curry a very unusual taste. For the vegetarians, the fish and prawns are replaced with Moong sprouts or Arbi vegetable (Taro root). The other specialty is the Mackerel curry with a special spice ingredient named Teppal or Triphal.

A New Chapter

Teppal or Triphal

This spice is mostly available and used in the west coast of India where it appears in fish dishes. Teppal is mostly used in fish and some vegetarian dishes, with a paste of coconut and chilies. While eating, teppal is not consumed but discarded. This spice has a pungent taste but goes best with Mackerel or sardine curry. It is also recommended that the smaller sized mackerel are best as far as the taste of the fish is concerned. It being pungent only three to four pieces of the Triphal spice is good enough in any preparation. Also, it should be lightly crushed and not blended into a paste. My Ajji was known for two more authentic mackerel recipes. One being the Udit Methi Mackerel recipe and the other called as 'Aamshetikshe'.

A Mother's Dream

Recipe No 8: Mackerel Triphal Curry
(Serves 2)

Ingredients
- 4 pcs Mackerel (medium size)
- 6 dry red chillies (Byadgi)
- 2 tbsp coriander seeds
- 2 tbsp tamarind paste
- ¼ tsp turmeric powder
- 10 triphal seeds
- 3 tbsp fresh grated coconut
- 1 tsp of pure coconut oil (optional)
- Water
- Salt

To serve with
- Steamed rice

Preparation
1) Grind to a paste the fresh grated coconut, red chillies, tamarind, turmeric powder, coriander seeds and water.
2) Place the Mackerels in a cooking pot and add the ground paste to it.
3) Add water to bring to curry like consistency.
4) Add salt.
5) Add triphal seeds (slightly crushed).
6) Bring to boil.
7) Once cooked garnish it with pure coconut oil.

Variation
One can replace mackerel with Tarle (Sardines) or Karli (Silver Bar Fish).

Cooking tip
Ensure the triphal is slightly crushed. Just run the triphal in a mixer grinder for 2-3 seconds. If you crush it more the curry will become very pungent.

A Mother's Dream

Recipe No 9: Udid Methi Mackerel
Serves 2

Ingredients
- 4 pcs Mackerel (medium size)
- 6 dry red chillies (Byadgi)
- 2 tbsp coriander seeds
- ¼ tsp methi (Fenugreek) seeds
- ½ tsp white urad dal
- ¼ tsp turmeric powder
- 5 petals of kokum or 1 ½ tbsp tamarind paste
- ½ cup fresh grated coconut
- ½ tsp of rice soaked in 1 tbsp water
- 2 tbsp pure coconut oil or any other cooking oil
- 1 small finely chopped onion
- 1 green chilli sliced
- Salt
- Water

Preparation
1) Heat pan and add ½ tbsp of oil.
2) Roast all ingredients (red byadgi chillies, turmeric powder, coriander seeds, urad dal, jeera and methi) separately and keep aside.
3) Grind the above roasted ingredients along with fresh grated coconut, tamarind and rice to a thick paste.
4) Heat pan and add 1 ½ tbsp of oil and lightly stir fry the onions and green chilli.
5) Add the ground paste to the pan.
6) Add water to make a semi thick consistent curry.
7) Add the mackerel, salt and bring to boil.
8) Serve with steamed rice.

Cooking Tip
One can either add tamarind (if available) while grinding the coconut or simply add the kokum petals to the curry while bringing it to boil.

A Mother's Dream

Recipe No 10: Aamshetikshe
(Serves 2)

Ingredients
- 4 pcs Mackerel (small or medium size)
- 2 tbsp pure coconut oil or any regular cooking oil
- 5 dry red chillies (Byadgi)
- 2 tbsp coriander seeds
- 1 ½ tbsp tamarind paste
- ¼ tsp turmeric powder
- 10 triphal seeds
- 1 tbsp fresh grated coconut
- 1 fresh haldi (turmeric) leaf (optional)
- Salt
- Water

Preparation
1) Grind to thick paste fresh grated coconut, red chillies, tamarind, turmeric powder and coriander seeds.
2) Apply the paste to the Mackerel and place in a broad based pan.
3) Add salt.
4) Place the haldi leaf in the pan along with the slightly crushed triphal seeds.
5) When done pour 1-2 tbsp pure coconut oil over the fish (optional).

Cooking tip
- Ensure the triphal is slightly crushed. Just run the triphal in a mixer grinder for 2-3 seconds. If you crush it more the curry will become very pungent.

- Do not add too much water. The dish is semi dry in consistency and hence should be cooked in a broad based pan.
- Fish gets very tender when cooked. So a broad based pan for this recipe will help in serving the fish as a whole piece.
- Small medium sized mackerels taste better than the big sized mackerels.

Variation
One can replace mackerel with Tarle (Sardines) or Karli (Silver Bar Fish).

Both the Mackerel recipes given above are very healthy in that these are oil free recipes. Also, fish is supposed to be healthy in terms of its nutritional value. On a lighter note, it is generally said, people who consume more fish are intelligent.

So, things were sort of settling down. Ajji with a steady job in Yellapur, my two aunts in Pune and my Maama in Kumta – each pursuing their school education. One morning, my Ajji got an urgent message to reach Kumta. It transpired that my Maama had been ill with fever for a long time and was diagnosed with Typhoid. He had become very weak and Hegde Uncle was concerned and had sent an urgent message to Ajji. So, my Ajji with my Mother reached Kumta. My Maama was really in bad shape, he was weak. It seems during that time they would keep cotton on the chest to figure out if he was still breathing or not. My Ajji, together with my Mother stayed in Kumta till the time my Maama recovered and gained some strength, and it was safe to get him to travel to Yellapur. With limited resources, the only way to travel was public state transport, which usually was with limited service and overcrowded. It was not possible to hire an ambulance. So, with the help of Hedge Uncle, they managed to convince the bus conductor to allocate a full berth on one of the trips, such that my Maama could sleep on the berth and travel comfortably. With a full berth booked, my Ajji along with my ailing Maama and my Mother started on their return journey to Yellapur.

On return to Yellapur, Maama took a while to recover fully to his routine. He needed lot of care. After my Maama

A New Chapter

recovered, my Ajji decided to let him continue his schooling in Yellapur for the next one year, until Grade Seven. During that time the schools in Yellapur had provision only till Grade Seven. Thereafter, those who aspired to pursue further studies had to move out from Yellapur for further schooling. So, my Maama had to move to Ankola (which was a distance place) to pursue education at the next level.

Life moved on while all the children continued with their secondary education. As usual it had its share of high and low phases. Both my aunts who were put up in the Boarding School in Pune would visit home once a year during the vacation time, even though they had two vacations a year, summer vacation in the month of May and the Diwali vacation. Ajji could afford to get them home only once in a year, which was typically the summer vacation. In the initial years Ajji would travel to Pune to bring them home and then again to drop them back to the Institute. As they grew older and became independent, they would travel on their own with the other Institute members. My Mother recalls that Ajji would look forward to have them home at Yellapur. She would prepare for their homecoming like for an upcoming festival. Months before their arrival, she would start preparing by ensuring the kitchen was stocked with sufficient supplies. This would typically mean setting aside groceries from the regular monthly supplies; cutting down on meals to save on ration and so on.

Some of the dishes that my aunts relished were 'Hinga Tamli' and 'Fish Curry' and 'Jeera Meera' egg curry. The egg curry was a special curry and was called the Jeera Meera Curry. The eggs would be substituted with tur dal on days when one did not consume eggs or for pure vegetarians.

During the mango season the girls would look forward to the raw mango curry and another dish made from ripe mango called 'Ambya Sasam". Ambya Sasam is a great combination with the regular yellow dal. Another specialty was the Bhendi Kadi, a curd-based lady finger curry.

A New Chapter

Recipe No 11: Hinga Tamli
(Serves: 2)

Ingredients
- 1 cup of fresh grated coconut
- 2 dry red chillies (Byadgi)
- ¼ tsp tamarind paste
- ¼ tsp of hing (Asafoetida)
- ½ tsp of ghee
- Salt
- Water

To serve with
- Steamed rice
- Fried fish

Preparation
1) Grind to paste fresh grated coconut, red chillies and tamarind.
2) Heat ghee in a pan and add the hing and roast it for a few seconds.
3) Add this to the paste and grind it for one last time.
4) Empty the paste in a bowl, add salt as per taste and add water to get the consistency of curry.
5) Serve with steamed rice and fried fish.

Note
- This is a raw curry and should not be boiled / heated.
- Since it is raw in nature consume it within a day or two and store in refrigerator. Alternatively freeze it if required to store for longer duration. Coconut used in raw form will go stale if not consumed within a day or two.

Recipe No 12: Fish Fry
(Serves 2)

Ingredients
- 4 fish fillet (any sea fish)
- 1 ½ tbsp of tamarind paste
- 1 ½ tbsp of chilli powder
- ½ tsp of turmeric powder
- ½ tsp coriander powder
- 50 gm of fine rava (semolina)
- 1 tbsp of rice flour
- 3 tbsp cooking oil for pan frying
- Salt

Preparation
1) Mix together to make a paste of tamarind pulp, chilli powder, turmeric and salt.
2) Apply paste to the fish fillet and marinate for 30 minutes.
3) In a plate mix the rava and rice flour. Place the marinated fish fillet (one at a time) on the rava. Flip it to ensure all sides are coated with the rava.
4) Heat pan and grease with oil.
5) Then place fish fillets on the pan.
6) Let it cook for 3-4 minutes on low flame. Turn flip the fish on the other side. Add oil and cook for 3-4 minutes.

Variation
- One can replace tamarind with 2 tbsp of lime juice.
- One can also add 1 tsp of garlic ginger paste to the marination.

Cooking Tip
- Rice flour helps to make the fish crispy when fried.
- Ensure you flip the fish with care to avoid it from breaking.
- Fish typically gets cooked in about 10 minutes.

Recipe No 13: Jeera Meera Egg Curry
(Serves 2)

Ingredients
- 1 cup fresh grated coconut
- 3 dry red chillies (Byadgi)
- 1 ½ tbsp coriander seeds
- 1 tsp of cumin seeds
- ½ tsp of peppercorns
- ¼ tsp turmeric powder
- 8 garlic cloves
- 2 tsp of ghee
- A leaflet of curry leaves
- 1 small onion finely chopped
- 1 small tomato finely chopped
- 1 tbsp coriander leaves finely chopped
- 3 kokum petals
- 3 eggs
- Salt
- Water

Preparation
1) Heat a pan and add 1 tsp of ghee.
2) Lightly stir fry the red chillies, coriander seeds, cumin, pepper, turmeric powder, garlic.
3) Grind to paste all the above along with fresh grated coconut.
4) Heat a broad-based deep cooking pot. Add ghee, onion, tomato, curry leaves and fry till slightly brown.
5) Add the ground paste and water to bring to desired curry consistency.
6) Add salt and kokum petals and boil for 3-4 minutes.

7) Crack an egg at a time in a small bowl and gently slip it into the boiling curry and let it cook for 30 seconds before adding the next egg.
8) Cook till the eggs are done.
9) Garnish with coriander leaves.
10) Serve with steamed rice.

Variation
One can replace the red chillies with green chillies.

Cooking tip
This is like a poached egg curry. Only ensure that the egg is fully cooked. It takes about 10 minutes for the eggs to get fully cooked.

Recipe No 14: Bhendi Kadi (Lady Finger) (Serves 2)

Ingredients
- 250 gm Bhendi (Lady Finger) diced
- ½ cup fresh grated coconut
- 3 green chillies
- 1 tbsp coriander seeds
- ½ tsp of cumin seeds
- ¼ tsp methi seeds (Fenugreek)
- 6 curry leaves
- ¼ tsp mustard seeds
- ¼ tsp hing (Asafoetida)
- ¼ tsp jeera
- ¼ tsp turmeric powder
- Sugar (one pinch)
- 4 kokum petals
- ½ to 1 cup thick butter milk
- 2 tbsp cooking oil
- Salt
- 1 glass of water

Preparation
1) Heat pan with 1 tbsp of cooking oil and lightly stir fry the green chillies, 1 tbsp of coriander seeds, ¼ tsp of cumin seeds and ¼ tsp of the methi seeds.
2) Grind the above with fresh grated coconut into fine paste
3) Heat the cooking pot and add 1 tbsp of oil. Add the curry leaves, Mustard seeds, cumin seeds, turmeric powder and hing.
4) Add bhendi and stir fry for 2 minutes.
5) Add 1 glass of water and cook for 5 minutes.

6) Once the bhendi is done add the ground paste, kokum petals and pinch of sugar and bring to boil.
7) Switch off the heat and add the butter milk. Do not boil after adding butter milk.
8) Add salt to taste and serve with steamed rice.

Recipe No 15: Raw Mango Ghashi (curry)
(Serves 2)

Ingredients
- 1 medium sized raw mango (diced into medium long pieces)
- ½ cup fresh grated coconut
- 3 green chillies
- 1 tbsp ginger paste
- 1 tbsp coriander seeds
- 1½ tbsp jaggery
- Salt as per taste
- Water as per consistency
- Coriander leaves finely chopped for garnishing.

For the tempering (tadka)
- 1 tbsp oil
- ½ tsp mustard seeds
- ½ tsp cumin seeds
- ½ tsp white urad dal
- A leaflet of curry leaves
- ¼ tsp turmeric powder
- ¼ tsp hing (asafoetida) powder

Preparation
1) Heat the pan for tempering (tadka). Put oil and add the mustard seeds, cumin seeds, methi seeds, turmeric, curry leaves and hing.
2) Add the diced raw mango pieces and some water to cover the pieces keep on slow flame till the mango pieces are cooked.
3) Blend together in a mixer the fresh grated coconut, green chillies, ginger paste, coriander seeds.

4) Add this paste to the mango, add water to get a curry like(medium thick) consistency, add jaggery, and salt and bring to boil.
5) Garnish with coriander leaves.

Recipe No 16: Ambya Sasam (Mango Raita) (Serves 2)

Ingredients
- One ripe mango de-skin and cut into small pieces
- ½ cup fresh grated coconut
- ¼ tsp mustard seeds
- 1 dry red chilli (Byadgi)
- ½ tbsp jaggery
- Salt
- Water

Preparation
1) Grind to paste the fresh grated coconut, mustard seeds, red chilli with litter water.
2) Add this to the cut mango and mash it slightly.
3) Add jaggery and salt as per taste.

My aunts recall that during their stay at the Pune Institute it was only once that they managed to visit home during the Diwali festival. The joy of celebrating Diwali at home as a family has left a lasting impression on all the siblings. The Diwali Day rituals (Day One) would typically mean getting up early in the wee hours, the lady of the family applying scented oil on the body and getting a hot water bath; which was later followed by prayers and the Diwali breakfast that the family had together. Apart from the regular Diwali savories that get prepared in all Indian families, the trade mark was hand crushed poha and a sweet dish called 'Mande'. This tradition of having a Diwali breakfast as a family has since then been carried forward till date. I have grown up hearing telephonic conversations between by Mother and aunts every Diwali during which they routinely share updates of all the traditional savories that they prepared during Diwali and fondly remembering their 'Amma' – my Ajji. My Maami too has ensured that she carried forward this ritual diligently.

A New Chapter

Recipe No 17: Mande
(Serves 10)

Ingredients

Dough
- 2 cups all-purpose flour (Maida)
- 2 tablespoon ghee melted
- Salt
- Water to make dough

Ingredients for stuffing
- 1 desiccated coconut
- 1 ½ cup powdered sugar
- 2 tablespoon sesame seeds (Til)
- 2 teaspoons green cardamom powder (Elaichi)

Deep Frying
- ½ L cooking oil

Preparation

Dough making
1) Add the flour to a mixing bowl, add salt and hot ghee and rub the ghee into the flour.
2) Add a little water at a time and knead to make a soft and smooth dough.
3) Cover the dough and allow it to rest for 20 - 30 minutes.

Prepare the stuffing
1) Heat a pan and add the desiccated coconut and stir until you get a roasted aroma.
2) Keep aside to cool completely.

3) In the same pan slightly roast the sesame seeds and let it cool completely.
4) In a bowl mix the desiccated coconut, sesame seeds, powdered sugar and cardamom powder.
5) Mix to combine all the ingredients well and keep aside.

Method to make the Mande
1) Preheat the oil in a deep-frying pan.
2) Divide the dough into 20 equal portions.
3) Dust in a little flour and roll out thin 5 to 6 inch diameter circles (size of a puri). Ensure to roll thin circles so that it does not puff up when deep fried.
4) Place the circles into the hot oil and fry either side for about 10 seconds until they begin to turn lightly golden brown.
5) Pull out the puri from the oil and immediately evenly sprinkle about a tablespoon of the coconut mixture over one half of the fried circle, then fold over the other half to form a semicircle.
6) Sprinkle a couple of more teaspoons of the sugar mixture over half the semicircle and fold over once more.
7) This folding and sprinkling of coconut mixture has to be done immediately after frying when the puris are soft. Once it gets cool, it becomes crispy and will break.
8) Repeat this process for rest of the remaining portions of the dough.
9) Store the Mande in an airtight container.

Cooking tip
- Step 6 above is optional. One can also do just one-fold
- It is suggested to roll out and keep ready all the dough circles before starting the frying process.
- Take additional help when you begin the frying process. One person can fry the circles and the other person can

A New Chapter

immediately sprinkle the coconut sugar and do the required folds.

It seems that every year, when my aunts would visit during the annual vacation, my Ajji would want to perform a Satyanarayana Puja before their departure. The puja was performed to seek God's blessing and for their safety. One of the family's well-wishers was a Brahmin couple known as the Bhatt family. They functioned as the village Pujaris and caretakers of the village temple. My Ajji, because of her good and sweet nature, had managed to build a very functional network full of bonhomie, with the people around her. She placed a premium on valuable relationships with the people around. Being a small place, all members of the village were well aware of the backgrounds and struggles of each family. The Bhatt family was attached to Ajji – whom they loving addressed as 'Bai Amma'. Every time my aunts were on vacation, the Bhatt family would take it upon themselves to ensure that the Satyanarayana Puja was performed. They would tell my Ajji, 'Bai Amma you don't worry. You just come and we will perform the Pooja. Have the Prasad and go back home satisfied. You don't spend anything. We will take care of the expenses."

My Maama and Mother recall that when my aunts would go back to the Pune Institute after the vacation, Ajji would weep and feel devastated for days. She would feel like she had deprived her children of a home. I have been brought to believe that my Ajji always carried around this baggage that she was not able to provide for a normal childhood to her children due to her poor financial condition.

A Mother's Dream

As life marched on its way forward, my Ajji was quite determined to ensure that her children would not have to face the same hardships as she had. Moreover, the importance of an appropriate education was always uppermost in her mind so that they should be able to only rise higher and higher in life. She was not one to settle for basic education. She was clear that she wanted to get them into professional courses. While my Maama was completing Grade Seven, she had made up her mind to move him to Ankola to complete his matriculation. And so, as she had pre-decided, my Maama was shifted to Ankola. He was about twelve or thirteen years old and was put in an accommodation where he survived on his own. He attended to the daily household chores, attended school and studied in his spare time. The distance between Yellapur and Ankola was of about an hour and a half. My Ajji would send across the ration to my Maama every month. And how do you think she managed this!? Well! My Ajji would pack all the required utilities and put my Mother on the bus to Ankola who was at that time around eight years old. And my Maama would meet her at the bus stop to collect the same and again see her off to Yellapur. In those days the bus drivers and conductors would take on the role of acting as guardians during the journey. They played the roles of postmen, delivery men and caretakers. My Ajji would send across letters through the driver informing my Maama about when she intended to send the ration so that he would make himself available to collect the ration.

A New Chapter

In the initial years my Maama was by himself; later on, during Grade Ten, he had a roommate. His name was 'Seshu' and we all grew up calling him Seshu Maama. He was like Ajji's second son and the bond only grew stronger. Seshu Maama was a native of Yellapur. He was known to the family as he and my Maama had attended the same school in Yellapur. Seshu Maama was junior to my Maama at school by two years. Like my Maama he too moved to Ankola to pursue matriculation and thus they landed up staying together as roommates. He too addressed my Ajji as 'Amma' meaning 'Mother' like the rest in the family. Seshu Maama became an integral part of the family. He joined the Department of Forest and served as a Civil Servant, Divisional Forest Officers (DFO) at the time of his retirement.

When I reflect on the myriad challenges faced by my family, the hardship, and how they faced obstacles, and cleared the path forward, my belief in the power of intention and faith only gets reinforced. The concept of the 'Law of Attraction' and the 'Power of the Universe' to serve you what you want, stands tested.

> *"In the universe there is an immeasurable, indescribable force which the shamans call intent, and absolutely everything that exists in the entire cosmos is attached to intent by connecting a link."*
> *— Carlos Castaneda*

5
Some New Relationships

"The moment one definitely commits oneself, then Providence moves too. All sorts of things occur to help one that would never otherwise have occurred...unforeseen incidents, meetings and material assistance, which no man could have dreamed would come his way."
— Johann Wolfgang von Goethe

I strongly believe in the above statement. I have experienced this in my personal life ever since I have learnt to live my life with a conscious mind. The very fact that I am writing this book is the proof of this principle. The right people show up in your life and play a role that enable the fulfilment of the situation at hand. Some people come in as good Samaritans and others evolve into deep relations as family and friends.

I relate an incident that my Maama often recalls, when he was in Grade Nine. He had not paid the school fees and hence his result was kept on hold. He did not have money and did not want to ask his Mother. Apparently, one of his classmates learnt about this situation. This classmate came from an established and economically secure background. He quietly arranged for the money and paid it on Maama's behalf in the school office. Later on, when Maama tried to repay the same, he refused to acknowledge that he had made any such payment and hence was not going to accept the money. Amazing! Isn't it? I am struck by the generosity of the gesture.

A Mother's Dream

The love and compassion that this classmate had developed at this young age to reach out to someone in need was remarkable and praiseworthy.

Another interesting or rather beautiful relationship blossomed during this time. While my aunts were growing up in the Karve Institute in Pune, the institute would be frequented by a gentleman called Mr. Manohar Gongolli. Whom my aunts referred to as 'Gaon Maama', which in literal sense meant 'Maama from hometown'. Gongolli Maama originally hailed from Karwar but settled in Pune with his wife and daughter. He was aware that the Karve Institute housed some students from Karwar districts; and out of general affection and care he would visit the institute regularly to meet with the students and to attend to their concerns. One may say, he was a self-appointed guardian of all the Karwar students placed in the Karve Institute. This relationship strengthened over time. Once Gaon Maama visited Yellapur and met up with my Ajji. And from that day onwards a new family bond was developed.

When my Maama and Mother moved to Pune to pursue higher studies and needed a temporary abode between admissions, Gaon Maama and Maami opened their home with large hearts and accepted them into their home. He happened to be a strong pillar during the years my Maama and my Mother were in Pune for studies. This relationship with Gongolli Maama and Maami has been cherished ever since. I recall my visit to their home as a child with my Mother. I recall meeting Gaon Maami and her daughter. Gaon Maama had passed away. Most of all, I have witnessed the fond exchange between Gaon Maami and my Mother. It was the same place that they continued to reside in. My Mother recalls, that during her nursing time, she would visit them often and had developed ties with the neighbourhood too. So, while she visited, she would also enquire about the neighbours and their whereabouts and progress as well.

So, my Maama was in Ankola, my aunts in Pune and my Ajji and my Mother in Yellapur. For Inter Science first year (which was after Matriculation) Maama moved to Dharwad and joined Karnatak College, and for Inter Science final moved to Lingaraj College in Belgaum.

Student life was a struggle. He had to manage with the limited resources – which meant at times that he ate just one meal a day. My Maama was blessed with some good friends during this phase of his life. He had one particular friend who showered him with warmth and generosity. My Maama recalls that during that time he did not have much liberty to have a carefree life. Money was always in short supply. His friends would love to eat out and would often invite Maama to join. But my Maama would not accept these invitations. He would plead with his friends that he should not be called as he could not afford to eat out. However, one particular friend, Gunkali, on frequent occasions would be stubborn, and forcefully get Maama to join them and would foot the entire bill.

Friendship is such a wonderful gift God has given to mankind. It is a blessing to be surrounded by truly genuine friends. I am sure you will agree with me that true friendship makes you feel like the richest person on this earth. I have grown up seeing some of these friendships growing stronger and building into close family ties. In fact, we have grown to treat these dear friends, who only wished us well, as family. It is a matter of great wonder, when now in their grey years, they take pride in celebrating their friendship.

A Mother's Dream

I remember one particular interaction with my Mother's best friend, Bandi Maushi. She said to me, "Nayana, do you know Summi (my Mother's maiden name is Sumitra and was called 'Summi' by friends and 'Mitra' by family members) and I have been friends for six decades!? It's such a beautiful thing. We have been having such a lovely time all through!!" In this moment, I recollect that beautiful poem on friendship by Khalil Gibran and would like to dedicate it to all our dear friends who were, and still continue to be, an integral part of our lives...

"And a youth said, Speak to us of Friendship.
And he answered, saying:
Your friend is your needs answered.
He is your field which you sow with love and reap with thanksgiving.
And he is your board and your fireside.
For you come to him with your hunger, and you seek him for peace.
When your friend speaks his mind you fear not the "nay" in your own mind, nor do you withhold the "ay."
And when he is silent your heart ceases not to listen to his heart;
For without words, in friendship, all thoughts, all desires, all expectations are born and shared, with joy that is unacclaimed.
When you part from your friend, you grieve not;
For that which you love most in him may be clearer in his absence, as the mountain to the climber is clearer from the plain.
And let there be no purpose in friendship save the deepening of the spirit.
For love that seeks aught but the disclosure of its own mystery is not love but a net cast forth: and only the unprofitable is caught.
And let your best be for your friend.

Some New Relationships

If he must know the ebb of your tide, let him know its flood also.
For what is your friend that you should seek him with hours to kill?
Seek him always with hours to live.
For it is his to fill your need but not your emptiness.
And in the sweetness of friendship let there be laughter, and sharing of pleasures.
For in the dew of little things the heart finds its morning and is refreshed."

By this time while my Maama was in his inter science final year my eldest aunt had finished her Grade Ten at Karve Institute and was back in Yellapur. Before one could decide on her next level of academic advancement, a marital alliance came up. Everything seemed perfect and it was decided to go ahead with the proposal. So immediately after Grade Ten my aunt Radha Pachi was given away in marriage; and very soon she moved to Hubli to settle into her new phase of life.

By this time, my Maama too had completed his Inter Science and was looking at pursuing an Engineering course. He applied for this course at the Pune Engineering College. At that point the only relation the family had outside Yellapur was that of Gaon Maama. He proved to be a great support (moral, emotional and at times financially) to help my Maama settle down in Pune for his Engineering studies.

I once asked my Maama, how he coped with his studies. He said, he managed to pull off his engineering exams with whatever was taught in the class. He said he had to be very attentive and register as much as he could and study only on that basis. He said, he had limited resources to spend on purchasing text books or workbooks. So, he had to ensure he registered all that was taught in class. He added, "How do you study if you have nothing to refer to? I would borrow study material from friends and refer to library books…"

In the coming year, my other aunt Sushil Pachi completed Matriculation. Sushil Pachi was academically very bright. She was a First Ranker in her class all through. After her Matriculation, arrangements were made and she was enrolled in the Karnataka College, in Dharwad to complete the next level.

So, by the time my Maama moved to his third year of engineering, my aunt had completed Inter Science. As she was so good at studies my Ajji was determined to get her into Medicine. So, on her own, my aunt managed to secure admission on merit, at the Hubli Medical College to pursue Medicine. So, you see, my Ajji's dreams were beginning to come true! She got two of her children to enrol in professional courses!

At around the same time my Mother her completed Matriculation. My Mother always considered herself fortunate enough to be under her mother's care all throughout her childhood. Being by her side has shaped her personality slightly differently. She was witness to all the hardships and vulnerable situations that Ajji had to experience first hand. All these experiences had her evaluate the circumstances and arrive at her conclusions on her path ahead. She was aware of the financial burdens of funding the education of my Maama and Aunt. She had resolved to extend her support by contributing financially. So, she had made up her mind to discontinue mainstream education and enroll for a nursing programme. The single largest factor that drove her to pursue nursing was the fact that nursing students

Some New Relationships

earned a stipend and all the expenses were taken care of by the Institute. She would thus be able to contribute to the finances and not put further burden on her Mother. My Ajji was reluctant but eventually gave in to my Mother's decision.

Ajji connected with Gaon Maama in Pune, who made enquiries at the Pune Sassoon Hospital. With his help my Mother landed in Pune and underwent the admission process. My Mother was a bright student too and managed to secure admission to the Nursing course at Sassoon. It seems from the time she secured admission to the start of the course there was a fifteen-day gap. During this time Gaon Maama extended shelter to my Mother at his residence. It was a selfless act of care and support extended by his entire family.

I recall from when I was around ten years old, they had a very humble living, while we had sort of attained a modest living compared to them. I remember the thoughts running in my mind. The place was very inconvenienced, but the people were very loving and were very fondly engaged in interacting with my Mother, only to realise years later the significant role they played in our lives. Our entire family will be forever indebted to Gaon Maama for generations to come. He and his family were the only anchor our family had with whom my Mother and Maama would connect without any hesitation. They extended tremendous emotional and moral support. To have someone whom you can rely on in an unknown city is a lifesaver. They were always greeted and welcomed with a smile and affection. With a lot of gratitude, I humbly pray for his soul to be in peace and achieve 'mukti'.

It was a new phase of life for both my Mother and Ajji. Of all the children, my Mother was the only one to have been by my Ajji's side and had witnessed all the physical hardships and emotional upheavals, and now after so many years had to part from her, for the first time. In a way, with my Mother also moving out, the family seemed to have become dismantled. My Maama and Mother in Pune were staying in independent hostels, one aunt was married away and another was in Hubli and my Ajji was by herself in Yellapur. However, there was the certainty that though the family members might have been physically apart, they always cherished bonds that could well be called unbreakable.

The Nursing course at Sassoon Hospital was all paid for – the tuition fee, uniform, stay and food plus the stipend of INR 30-40 per month. This course duration was of three and a half years, after which, based on merit, the candidate would be posted to a government hospital.

My Mother recalls how adjusting to the city life was a task. Yellapur was a small village, where electric supply was a rare thing. She recalls, when she first came to Pune – she did not know how to work the switch buttons, to put the lights and fans on and off. Language was also an issue. She had to cope with the local language Marathi, and English in the classrooms. From the stipend amount, she would retain a small amount for herself to meet basic sundry expenses and the rest she would pass on to my Maama to aid his education expenses.

Both my Ajji and Maama were not very happy with my Mother's decision to quit mainstream education. My Mother was good at academics. All of them saw the diversion as a passing phase and were determined that she moved back into mainstream. Working at the hospital definitely exposed my Mother to all kinds of situations and human interactions.

Some New Relationships

Her first delight of moving to the city was the introduction to electricity. Those residing in the cities were privileged to experience the comfort of having the fans and tube lights and bulbs light up in their houses during the early morning and evening time and not manoeuvre their way with kerosene lanterns or oil lamps.

My Mother remembers a hilarious incident at the Sassoon Hospital. Being new to city life, she was also getting accustomed to technology. Her introduction to using the telephone was a nasty one. She was not aware of how to use the telephone. On one instance, while she was in the ward, the telephone rang, and for the first time she answered the call. The caller requested to speak with the doctor. My Mother, without checking on the caller's details or anything said ok and went to fetch the Doctor. When the Doctor came and asked where the call was, she simply pointed to the telephone. She was not aware that she had to place the receiver alongside the telephone. My Mother had happily put the receiver back on the telephone not knowing that she had actually disconnected the call. She recalls the earful she had received for this disaster.

A Mother's Dream

Some New Relationships

My Mother made good friends with who were accustomed to city life and ensured that she came up the curve in a short span of time. She very fondly remembers her friends, Shashikala Belekar and Shaila Kotak. Belekar aunty taught my Mother to ride the bicycle in the crowded lanes of the Pune Lakshmi Market. My Mother recalls, how her friend Belekar would zoom off on her bicycle and that she was left with no choice but to catch up with the speed. My Mother gives Belekar aunty all the credit for teaching her to ride the bicycle. Both Belekar aunty and Shaila aunty continued with the nursing profession till their retirement.

My Mother recalls that she would often see a soft-spoken lady interact with Doctors and patients and their families. It was obvious to gauge from the interactions that this lady was spoken to with a lot of respect and she came across as very approachable. My Mother was very curious to know who she really was. On enquiring she learnt that she was Mrs. Dravid, who was a Medical Social Worker. Her role was to work with patients and their families in need of psychosocial help. My Mother always recalls that this incident made a lasting impact on her mind that motivated her to pursue her profession in Social Work.

While things were sort of settling down, some family challenges cropped up in the lives of my aunt Radha Pachi, who was married and blessed with three kids. Her husband turned to vices which made it difficult for the family to meet their basic requirements. This came as a terrible shock to my Ajji and Maama. My aunt, because of her limited qualification, was not able to support herself. My Ajji could not tolerate witnessing their misery. All means of rehabilitation proved futile and reluctantly my aunt and her kids had to be moved back to the maternal home. This added to the burden and took its toll on everyone involved as it was important to re-settle the disrupted life of my aunt and her children. Having said that, the responsibility was taken on wholeheartedly. My Maama, Sushil Pachi and Mother having taken life lessons and strength from my Ajji, wholeheartedly took on the responsibility of my aunt Radha Pachi and her children.

Like any Mother, my Ajji wanted the best for her children. She wanted them to be well fed, well dressed and well educated. She would visit my aunt at Hubli while she pursued medicine. On one such visit she happened to interact with all my aunt's friends. And she noticed that all her friends were comparatively well dressed and wore modest gold jewellery (like earrings, a chain and bangles). The incident made an impression; and she realised that my aunt needed a change in her wardrobe and accessories in order to match up to the level of her friends. The thought was not to compete with her friends – but seen as an inspiration to model the good in others and create a sense of oneness with them.

When I reflect on some of these instances, my admiration for my Ajji for her determination and foresight to live a complete life only increases. She, in the true sense of the term, is a 'Woman of Substance'. A lot of self-help books speak of developing the aspect of living in the company of achievers and positive neighbours. The first step in realising one's true vision is to identify with the traits of people one wants to be with or be like. And I guess that's exactly what my Ajji tried to do. And in doing so she ensured that her children moved on the right path.

Some of the delicacies that my aunt remembers are the finger licking chutneys that my Ajji would make. Penning down some of them with variations. For instance, the garlic cloves can be replaced with a one-inch piece of ginger to make ginger chutney. Or add a half cup of raw mango to make mango chutney. To give more flavour to the chutney one can give it a regular Tadka. In which case once the chutney is ready, take a tadka pan and heat a bit of oil; add one fourth tsp of Mustard seeds, cumin seeds, Hing and four to five curry leaves and pour the tadka over the chutney preparation.

Recipe No 18: Garlic Chutney
(Serves 2)

Ingredients
- 1 cup fresh grated coconut
- 1 dry red chilli (byadgi)
- ¼ tsp tamarind paste
- 8 garlic cloves
- Salt
- 1 pinch sugar
- ½ cup water

Preparation
1) Mix all ingredients (coconut, red chili, tamarind, garlic cloves) in a mixer jar. Add a little water and coarsely grind it.
2) Add salt and sugar as per taste.

Recipe No 19: Cucumber Chutney
(Serves 2)

Ingredients
- 2-3 cucumbers chopped very finely (squeeze to remove all water)
- ¼ cup fresh grated coconut
- 2 green chillies – medium size
- ½ dry red chilli broken into two pcs
- ¼ tsp jeera
- ½ tsp mustard
- ¼ tsp hing powder (Asafoetida)
- A leaflet of curry leaves
- ½ tsp cooking oil
- Salt
- Sugar (as per taste)
- ¼ tsp tamarind paste
- ½ cup water

Preparation
1) Take oil in pan and fry chili, jeera, ¼ tsp mustard and hing. Coarsely grind this with tamarind and fresh grated coconut.
2) In a bowl add the above and the cucumber and mix well.
3) Add salt and sugar as per taste.
4) Prepare for tempering. Heat oil in a tempering pan. Add the red chili, mustard & curry leaves and pour over the cucumber.

Variation
One can add 2 tbsp of curds as per taste.

Recipe No 20: Sweet and sour Mango chutney
(one of my favourites)
(Serves 2)

Ingredients
- 2 cups raw mango (de-skin and diced)
- 1 green chili (finely chopped)
- 1 tsp mustard seeds
- 1 tsp cumin seeds
- ¼ tsp hing (Asafoetida)
- A leaflet of curry leaves
- 1 tbsp oil
- Salt
- ¼ cup jaggery
- ½ cup water

Preparation
1) Take a shallow pan. Heat oil.
2) Add mustard seeds, cumin seeds, hing, curry leaves and green chili and stir.
3) Add the raw mango, ½ cup water and cook.
4) When mango is cooked add jaggery and cook till it dissolves.
5) Serve at room temperature.

Note
This chutney can be stored in refrigerator up to 3 weeks.

Recipe No 21: Dry prawn chutney
(Serves 2)

Ingredients
- ½ cup fresh grated coconut
- 2 dry red chilli (Byadgi)
- ¼ tsp tamarind paste
- 5 garlic cloves
- 1 cup dry prawns roasted
- 1 medium onion finely chopped
- Salt
- ½ cup water

Preparation
1) Coarsely grind fresh grated coconut, red chilli, tamarind, garlic cloves with a little water in a mixer jar.
2) Place the dry roasted prawns in a bowl and hand crush the dry prawns.
3) Add onions and the grounded paste and mix well.
4) Add salt as per taste.

Recipe No 22: Karela (Bitter gourd) Chutney (Serves 2)

Ingredients
- ½ cup fresh grated coconut
- 1 green chili
- ¼ tsp tamarind paste
- 1 piece of Karela (size of amla*)
- Salt
- ½ tsp sugar
- ½ cup water

Preparation
1) Lightly dry roast the karela in pan.
2) Coarsely grind to paste the fresh grated coconut, green chilli, tamarind and karela with a little water.
3) Transfer the mix in a bowl and add salt and sugar as per taste.

Note
*Indian Gooseberry

Talking about Karela (Bitter gourd) I recall, like most people I would run away from this vegetable. I would wonder what kind of taste people who enjoyed this vegetable had! I acquired my liking for this vegetable from my Ajji. This vegetable is supposed to be consumed for good health especially for those suffering from Diabetes. My Ajji was diabetic and hence this vegetable was part of her regular diet. One of the ways that she consumed this was by simply cutting the vegetable in slices, applying a bit of salt and a pinch of sugar and roasting it on tawa (pan). Three more of her karela specialties were a semi dry karela vegetable, Karela Ghashi and Karela Amshitikshe.

Recipe No 23: Karela Ghashi
(Serves 2)

Ingredients
- 100 gm karela (cut into fine round slices)
- 4 ambade / Hog Plum (de-skin)
- ½ cup grated coconut
- 1 ½ tbsp jaggery
- Salt
- Water

Main Masala (dry roast)
- 1 tbsp coriander seeds
- ½ tsp cumin seeds
- ¼ tsp fenugreek (methi seeds)
- 4 dry red chillies (Byadgi)

Tempering (Tadka)
- 2 tbsp oil
- ¼ tsp mustard seeds
- ¼ tsp cumin seeds
- ¼ tsp turmeric powder
- ¼ tsp hing (asafoetida)
- A leaflet of curry leaves

Preparation
1) Dry roast the main masala.
2) Grind to a smooth paste the fresh grated coconut along with the main masala and keep aside.
3) Heat pan for tempering. Add the ingredients one after the other in the order given under tempering above.

4) Add chopped karela and ambade and stir fry for 2 minutes.
5) Add water to cover the karela and ambade and cook for 10 minutes.
6) Add the ground paste and jaggery and bring to boil.
7) Add salt to taste.
8) Serve with rice.

Variation
- Ambade (Hog Plum) can be replaced with ½ cup of raw mango diced into small pieces.
- In case Ambade or raw mango is unavailable one can add 4 kokum petals or 1 tsp tamarind.

Cooking Tip
This preparation is sweet and sour in taste and hence one needs to add jaggery as per taste.

Recipe No 24: Karela Amshetikshe
(Serves 4)

Ingredients
- 250 gm karela (finely chopped)
- 2 tbsp tamarind paste
- 2 tbsp jaggery
- Water
- Salt

Main Masala
- 1-2 tsp of red chilli powder
- 1 tbsp coriander powder
- ½ tsp of cumin powder

Tempering (tadka)
- 2 tbsp cooking oil
- ½ tsp mustard seeds,
- ½ tsp cumin seeds
- ¼ tsp fenugreek (methi seeds)
- ¼ tsp turmeric powder
- ¼ tsp hing (asafoetida)
- A leaflet of curry leaves

Preparation
1) Heat pan for tempering. Add the ingredients one after the other in the order given under tempering above.
2) Add karela and stir fry for 2 minutes.
3) Add jaggery.
4) Add water to sufficiently cover the karela and cook for 5 minutes.
5) Add the main masala and tamarind pulp and bring to boil.

6) Ensure to have a thick gravy consistency.
7) Add salt to taste.

Note
This dish is served with rice or chapati.

Recipe No 25: Karela vegetable
(Serves 4)

Ingredients

- 250 gm Karela sliced into long thin strips
- 250 gm Potato sliced into long strips
- 200 gm onion finely chopped
- 300 gm tomato finely chopped
- 5-6 garlic cloves (crushed)
- 2 tsp red chilli powder
- ¼ tsp turmeric powder
- 1 tsp coriander powder
- ½ tsp of cumin powder
- ½ tsp garam Masala
- 12 tbsp of oil
- Salt
- 1 tsp sugar (as per taste)
- 3 tbsp chopped coriander leaves

Preparation

1) Heat 4 tbsp of oil in a pan and stir fry the Karela and potato till done and keep aside.
2) Take a broad based pan, add the oil and stir fry the finely chopped onions and crushed garlic till it turns slight brown.
3) Add the tomato and continue stirring to get a pulp like texture.
4) Add the turmeric powder, red chilli powder, coriander powder, cumin powder and garam masala and continue to stir for 5 minutes.
5) Add the fried karela and potato and stir in to mix well.
6) Add the salt and sugar as per taste.
7) Garnish with coriander leaves.
8) Serve with chapati or paratha.

A Mother's Dream

By this time, 1965, my Maama, Aunt (Sushil Pachi) and Mother were on the verge of attaining financial stability. It was decided that once the basic household was settled, my Ajji would quit her job and move to Mumbai for good. They continued like this for about three to four years, before being re-united in the city that welcomes and accommodates one and all. The city of the deity "Mumba Devi", the city where people across India aspire to live in order to fulfil their dreams – Bombay. Now known as Mumbai.

My Maama moved to Mumbai first, after completing his B.E. He got a job with Bhabha Atomic Research Centre (BARC). In the initial days his friend Mr. Mahajan from Mumbai extended his hospitality. So, my Maama could get accustomed to the 'Bambaiyya lifestyle'. Very soon he rented an apartment in Kumbar wada, Sindhi colony in Chembur. At this time, my Ajji was transferred to a place called Banavsi and my Aunt (Radha Pachi) and her 3 kids had moved in with my Ajji.

My Maama recalls an incident. The entire family had always managed with the bare minimum. It seems until he started earning, none in the family ever owned any pure silk garments. He gradually started ensuring that his sisters were provided with the traditional silk looms sarees. And eventually he managed to gather a decent collection for them. At that time my Aunt – Sushil Pachi was still pursuing Medicine and lived in the hostel. She had a decent collection of silk sarees by then. One day to her utter shock she found that all her silk sarees were gone. It seems, someone had been eyeing them for a while; and one fine day, her suitcase with all her precious collection just vanished. My Maama recalls, how Sushil Pachi came back home crying over her lost possessions and Maama had to take her shopping to console her.

My Mother recalls, that during festive seasons there would be discounts offered in the Co-Optex stores in Mumbai. These stores were known to sell traditional handlooms and they could accompany my Maama to select sarees of their choice. My Mother recalls with a lot of affection, how her brother would ensure that his sisters and Mother were dressed with the choicest of traditional handloom. This ritual of going shopping during the festive season was also a beginning of preparing for the wedding trousseau for my Aunt and Mother.

Eventually, my Ajji quit her job and moved to Mumbai for good. In the initial days they were staying at Kumbhar wada in Chembur Sindhi Colony. It was a one room kitchen household. A few months later my Mother joined them in Mumbai. She had cleared her nursing course and had topped her class. In those days, the Nursing Institute would make the student's placements based on grades. She was placed with the JJ Hospital in Mumbai. And thus, began life in Mumbai for the threesome. My Mother recalls, that every morning my Ajji would wake up early and have the meal ready by 7 am. It was a routine that my Maama and Mother had to have a wholesome home cooked meal before they left home for work. In addition, they would carry a lunch box. Eating meals in hotels was a complete 'No' for reasons of hygiene and expense. They would look forward to reach home to relish the warm home cooked food kept ready in the evening. A few months after my Mother moved to Mumbai, my Aunt also completed her MBBS and moved to Mumbai. She was posted at the Bhabha Hospital.

A Mother's Dream

Eventually, my eldest aunt, Radha Pachi, also moved to Mumbai with her three children. As things were getting difficult for her and the children with her difficult marriage. This did put pressure on the household but all in the household took joint responsibility to settle the issues. It was important to make my aunt Radha Pachi self-reliant. Her educational journey was re-installed and she was encouraged to pursue her next levels. Her journey began and she eventually completed her graduation and B.Ed and pursued a career as a Language teacher in Marathi and Hindi in a School in Camp area, Chembur.

My Mother continued working as a nurse for a period of two years. As things started getting a bit normal my Ajji and Maama pushed my Mother to pursue her academic journey. They were keen that my Mother pursued mainstream education and take up a professional course. So, my Mother left the nursing profession and took admission at Khalsa college to complete her Inter. During the course of this year, there was a marriage alliance and she had to take a break. However, she was determined to live up to the wish and desire of fulfilling her Mother's dream. Marriage, followed by child birth, resulted in a temporary break in her academic pursuits. However, she eventually enrolled for a distance graduation from Shreemati Nathibai Damodar Thackersey (SNDT) University in Arts followed by Master of Arts in Sociology. Things did not stop here. Her long-term aspiration was to pursue MSW – the Medical Social Worker at Sassoon who had been her inspiration. So, she waited patiently for things to fall in place. After I was born and started my play school years, she went ahead to complete her Masters in Social Work from College of Social Work, Nirmala Niketan, Mumbai.

Some New Relationships

Life in Mumbai moved on. The family expanded with all her children getting married and pursuing their dreams towards making life worthwhile. She was blessed with numerous grandchildren, thirteen to be precise. As I matured in life and began to connect with my Mother, more as a friend than a Mother, I have heard her share of my Grandmother's stories of struggle and her dreams for her children. She has always admired my Ajji for her courage, her aspirations and her dreams and her zeal to work towards them. Her persistent nature, her ability to accept the adversities of life and to stand strong have been a strong inspiration for me. The importance of education and self-reliance was so strong that Ajji ensured that her daughter-in-law, Shobha (my Maami), was also extended this opportunity to complete her education.

My Maami credits the completion of her graduation and B.Ed to my Ajji and Maama. When she joined the family, she had completed her matriculation. But the live wires of the household so focused on education and financial independency encouraged her to pursue her further studies. She recalls the days when she would finish the house work with my Ajji's support and then get into the quiet space, which was the building terrace to concentrate on her studies without being disturbed. In her absence, my Ajji would hold the fort on the home front. She fondly recalls an incident, when she was preparing for her B.Ed course, as part of the course fulfilment she had to prepare for classroom session that she had to present to a class. So, her rehearsal audience at home would be my Ajji, Maama and the kids, whom she had to teach.

Another episode that my Maami narrates and we all have a hearty laugh over, is about my Ajji's tenderness and gullible nature that empathized with the mothers of children who were academically weak. My Maami too pursued a career as a teacher. She taught English, Mathematics and Social Studies to Grades Nine and Ten. During the mid-term exams paper correction, she would narrate examples of how some students had fared badly in her subjects and were scoring low marks to the extent that they would have to repeat the year. It seems my Ajji would be in tears hearing about these cases and would plead with my Maami to re-evaluate their papers properly to ensure she had corrected them properly. She would sulk saying that, "their mothers will be pained to see their child's poor performance." She would be so disturbed that after a point my Maami decided to stop narrating such instances to her and avoid any further heartburns. My Maami is an amazing cook too, but she relishes some of Ajji's delicacies.

Some New Relationships

Recipe No 26: Kholumbo
(A variation of Sambar)
Serves 2

Ingredients
- 1 cup tur dal
- 2 tbsp grated coconut
- 1 small tomato (finely chopped boil it with the dal)
- 1 cup eggplant (diced)
- 1 drumstick (cut in 4 pieces)
- 1 ½ tbsp tamarind paste
- 1 ½ tbsp jaggery
- 2 tbsp chopped coriander leaves
- 1 tsp rice (soak in 1tbsp water)
- Salt
- 6 cups water

Main Masala
- 3 dry red chillies (Byadgi)
- 1 ½ tbsp coriander seeds
- ½ tsp cumin seeds
- ¼ tsp methi seeds (Fenugreek)
- 6 pepper corns
- 3 cloves
- ¼ tsp hing (asafoetida)
- ¼ tsp of cinnamon
- ¼ tsp turmeric powder
- 1tsp chana dal and udit dal each

Tempering (tadka)
- 2 tbsp cooking oil / Ghee
- ½ tsp mustard seeds

- ½ tsp cumin seeds
- ¼ tsp turmeric powder
- ¼ tsp hing (asafoetida)
- A leaflet of curry leaves

To serve with
- Rice
- Dosa
- Idli

Preparation
1) Pressure cook the tur dal with 3 cups of water and keep aside.
2) In another cooking pot cook the eggplant and drumstick till it is done. Do not overcook.
3) Heat 1 tsp of oil in a and roast all the ingredients under the main masala.
4) Grind to a paste all the main masala along with the grated fresh coconut, 1 tsp of rice (soaked in water) and tamarind.
5) Transfer the pressure cooked tur dal to a cooking pot.
6) Add the cooked eggplant and drumstick to the tur dal and stir well.
7) Add the ground paste and water to bring to desired consistency.
8) Add salt and jaggery as per taste and boil for 3-4 minutes.
9) Heat a tempering pan and add all the ingredients under tempering one after the other and pour the tempering over the dal.
10) Garnish with coriander leaves.

Some New Relationships

The same zeal and grit run in my Maama and my Mother, who have time and again stood as strong pillars and as guardians and protectors of the household. Some of Ajji's traits could be summarized as follows:
1. The Zeal to live life fully
2. Perseverance
3. Never give up attitude
4. Compassion for fellow beings and the passion to reach out for those in need
5. Adaptive and accommodative nature
6. Stop complaining and start living

'Education' as a basis for gaining self-reliance has been so strongly embedded in the mind that we as children are given all the support and opportunity to help us excel in academics and other life aspirations.

My memories of Ajji, like all grandparents have showered us with unconditional love. Though we are thirteen grandchildren to Ajji she has loved us without any partiality and favouritism – a very simple lady with a fair complexion, always decently clad is a simple sari. She would never tuck her sari pleats with safety pins. She had greyed very early in life. In brief, very simple and elegant. She was very fond of knitting and as kids we have been dressed up with her warm designer collection. It was not that she was trained in it. Knitting and Crochet came to her naturally. She would just look at patterns /designs and create something nice. She was able to knit one adult sweater in ten to fifteen days. She was so good at it, that she would knit a baby sweater in a matter of a few hours. My eldest aunt, Radha Pachi has picked up this artistic trait from her. And we have been passing on our demands to her.

A Mother's Dream

Old time memories were of the festive season, the festival of lights – Diwali. On the first day of Diwali – all my aunts, uncles and cousins would be invited over for the famously now missed Diwali lunch. It used to be time for fun and frolic. All cousins together involved in fun and laughter and sometimes our childish fights. My Maami would be the head cook and would serve us finger licking traditional delicacies. Most of the food cooked would be non-vegetarian and the regular Diwali savouries. Some of the delicacies are presented next.

Some New Relationships

Recipe No 27: Tisre Masala (clams)
(Serves 2)

Ingredients
- ½ kg clams (boiled and half of the shell retained)
- 1 cup grated coconut
- 1 small onion finely chopped
- 1 small tomato finely chopped
- A leaflet of curry leaves
- 6 roasted garlic cloves
- 1 ½ tbsp coriander leaves finely chopped
- 3 tbsp pure coconut oil or any cooking oil
- Salt
- 1 ½ cup water
- 1 tea spoon of rice soaked
- 5 kokum petals

Main Masala
- 4 dry red chillies (Byadgi)
- 1 ½ tbsp coriander seeds
- ½ tsp cumin seeds
- ¼ tsp methi (Fenugreek) seeds
- ¼ tsp turmeric powder
- 6 pepper corns
- 4 cloves
- 3 green cardamom
- ¼ tsp of cinnamon powder

Preparation
1) Heat pan and roast with a little oil all the main masala (one at a time) and grind to powder.
2) In a pan heat the pure coconut oil.

3) Add the onions, tomatoes, curry leaves and stir till light brown.
4) Add the clams and 1 cup water and let it cook for 5 minutes.
5) Coarsely grind to paste the fresh grated coconut, main masala, roasted garlic and the soaked rice.
6) Add this paste to the clams and stir with some water to get semi thick dry consistency.
7) Add kokum petals and salt to taste and boil for ten minutes.
8) Garnish with chopped coriander leaves.
9) Serve with steamed rice or neer dosa.

Variation
- Clams (Tisre) can be replaced with ½ kg oysters (either Khubbe or Kalwa) or two crabs or 250 gm prawns.
- However, do not retain the shell of the oyster in cooking. Boil the oyster and separate the shell from the meat. Use only the oyster meat.
- Clean crabs and separate the claws and centre piece and steam it with ½ cup water.

Recipe No 28: Mutton Curry
(Serves 4)

Ingredients
- 500 gm goat meat
- 3 medium onions finely chopped
- 3 medium tomatoes finely chopped
- 1 ½ tbsp ginger garlic paste
- 2 tbsp of red chilli powder
- ¼ tsp turmeric powder
- 2 tsp poppy seeds
- ½ tsp cumin powder
- ½ tsp coriander powder
- 1 cup fresh grated coconut
- 2 bay leaves
- 5 tbsp oil
- 2 tbsp coriander leaves finely chopped
- 2 tbsp pure ghee
- Salt
- 1 glass (250 mL) water

Garam masala
- 3 cloves
- 5 peppercorns
- 2 green cardamom
- 1 black cardamom
- 1 inch cinnamon stick
- 1 star anise
- 1 mace
- ¼ nutmeg
- 1 tsp fennel seeds
- ¼ tsp black cumin (Shah jeera)

Preparation

1) Heat a thick bottom pan. Add 3 tbsp of oil, bay leaves and half the onions and stir still light brown.
2) Add the tomatoes and stir for 5 minutes.
3) Add the mutton, 1 cup water and cook till done.
4) While the meat is getting cooked prepare to process the other ingredients.
5) Dry roast all the ingredients mentioned in the garam masala (one at a time) and grind it to powder in a mixer.
6) Heat a pan and the remaining cooking oil. Add onion and ginger garlic paste and stir for 2 minutes.
7) Add the fresh grated coconut, turmeric, poppy seeds, cumin coriander powder, chili powder, turmeric, garam masala powder, poppy seeds, cumin and coriander powder and stir for 3minutes. Set aside for it to cool.
8) Grind this in a mixer to make a fine paste.
9) Add the paste to the mutton. Salt as per taste and boil for 5 minutes.
10) Once done add the ghee and garnish with coriander leaves.

To serve with
- Steamed rice
- Neer dosa
- Soft dosa

Variation
- One can also make a semi solid mutton masala using the same ingredients. The difference is in step seven, where all the masalas except the fresh grated coconut have to be grounded to a fine paste and added to the mutton and boiled for 10 minutes. Coarsely grind the fresh grated coconut separately. Add this to the mutton and boil for 5 minutes.

- The mutton curry can be served with rice, dosa, or millet rotis.
- For those who do not consume red meat, this can be replaced with chicken or prawns.
- One can also add 2 medium sized potato (diced in large pieces) when the meat is half done. Add the potato when the meat is half done to avoid the potato getting overcooked.

Cooking tip

Garam masala is readily available in the market. However, making it fresh at home as per the recipe above adds to the aromatic flavour.

Recipe No: 29 Layered Mutton Biryani
(Serves 5)

Ingredients

Rice
- 3 glasses (750 gm) basmati rice
- 2 bay leaves
- 8 peppercorns
- 5 cloves
- 1 black cardamom
- 2 tbsp cooking oil
- 6 glasses of water

Mutton Gravy
- 750 gm goat meat
- 500 gm tomato
- 500 gm onions
- 250 gm potato
- 100 gm garlic
- 3 tbsp coriander seeds
- 2 tbsp chilli powder
- ¼ tsp turmeric powder
- 200 mL refined oil
- Salt
- Water

Garam masala (dry roast and powder)
- 3 cloves
- 5 peppercorns
- 2 green cardamom
- 1 black cardamom

- 1 inch cinnamon stick
- 1 star anise
- 1 mace
- ¼ nutmeg
- ½ tsp fennel seeds
- ¼ tsp black cumin seeds (shah jeera)

Biryani Layering
- 1 large onion sliced finely in length
- 2 tbsp cooking oil
- 3 boiled eggs sliced (optional)
- 1 cup fried cashew nuts (optional)
- 3 tbsp pure ghee
- 1 cup deep fried onions*(optional)
- 3 tbsp coriander leaves finely chopped

To serve with
- Onion tomato raita
- Fried papad

Preparation

Rice
1) Wash rice and drain water and keep aside for 10 mins.
2) Take a deep heavy broad based pan. Add 2 tbsp oil, bay leaves, cloves, pepper corns and green cardamom.
3) Add rice and stir for 2 minutes. Ensure to stir with delicate movement to avoid the rice from breaking into small pieces.
4) Boil 6 glasses of water and add it to the rice and cook till rice is 3/4th done.
5) Ensure the rice remains grainy and not mushy.

6) Cool the rice completely and fluff it to let the moisture evaporate out.

Meat gravy
1) Cook goat meat separately till it is 3/4th done.
2) Grind garlic and coriander seeds with very little water.
3) Heat the 200 mL cooking oil in a pan. Add the garlic and coriander paste and keep stirring till the paste turns brown.
4) Add turmeric powder and onions and continue to stir fry for 10 minutes.
5) Add chopped tomatoes and continue to stir fry for 5 minutes.
6) Add garam masala powder and stir for 5 minutes.
7) Add the 3/4th cooked goat meant and salt and bring to boil till the meat is fully cooked.

Setting the Biryani Layers
1) Take a broad based heavy bottom deep pan.
2) Pour 2 tbsp of cooking oil in the bottom of the pan and spread evenly.
3) Spread the sliced onions over the oil.
4) Now start putting the layers. 1st put a thin layer of rice and then a layer of the mutton gravy. Ensure the rice and mutton gravy is spread evenly.
5) Place a few pieces of the sliced eggs and few cashew nuts. Cover with a layer of rice, followed by mutton gravy, sliced eggs and cashew nuts.
6) Continue till you have some portion of rice left to put the final layer.
7) Garnish on top with the fried onion and chopped coriander leaves.
8) Melt the 2 tsbp of ghee and pour it evenly on the top.
9) Cover with a heavy lid. Alternatively keep a grinding

stone on the lid if available.
10) Keep the pan on low flame for 20-25 mins.

Note
*Long slice the onion, add a pinch of oil and mix. Squeeze out the oil and deep fry.

Variation
For those who do not consume red meat, this can be replaced with chicken or medium sized prawns.

Recipe No 30: Coconut rice
(Serves 2)

Ingredients
- 1 ½ cup basmati rice / normal rice
- 1 dry red (byadgi) chili (cut into 2-3 pieces)
- 4 tbsp pure coconut oil or any other cooking oil
- 1 tbsp chana dal
- ½ cup ground nuts
- ½ tsp jeera
- ½ tsp mustard seeds
- ½ tsp udit dal
- ¾ cup fresh grated coconut
- A leaflet of curry leaves
- 2 tbsp coriander leaves finely chopped
- Salt
- 3 cups water

Preparation
1) Wash rice and keep aside for 10 mins.
2) Add 3 cups of water to the rice and cook till done.
3) Ensure the rice remains grainy and not mushy.
4) Cool the rice completely and fluff it to let the moisture evaporate out.
5) Heat pan and add 2 tbsp of oil and fry the chana dal and peanuts and stir and keep aside.
6) Heat the remaining oil in the pan for tempering. Add udit dal, mustard seeds, jeera, red chilli and curry leaves. Stir for a while and add the Chana dal and peanuts.
7) Add the rice and stir for 2-3 minutes.
8) Add the grated coconut and salt as per taste and mix well.
9) Garnish with coriander leaves.

Recipe No 31: Patole (Steamed Rice Rolls) (Serves 2)

Ingredients

Dough
- 1 cup rice flour
- 3 cups of water
- 1 pinch of salt
- 1 tbsp of ghee

Filling
- 1 cup of grated coconut
- 1 cup of jaggery
- ½ tsp cardamom (elaichi) powder
- ¼ tsp nutmeg powder
- 1 tbsp of ghee
- 4 small fresh turmeric leaves

Preparation

Dough
1) Heat 3 cups of water in a vessel.
2) Add ghee, salt and add the rice flour and mix well. Keep aside for cooling.
3) Knead the mixture into a smooth dough.
4) Make into 4 portions and keep aside.

Filling
Heat pan and add ghee, fresh grated coconut, jaggery, cardamom and nutmeg powder and stir for 2 minutes. Keep aside.

Making the Patole
1) Take one leaf and coat it with very little ghee.
2) Spread one portion of dough evenly on the leaf.
3) On half the portion spread the coconut filling.
4) Cover the filling with the remaining half of the leaf.
5) Follow the process with the remaining 3 portions of the dough.
6) Place it in pressure cooker and steam for 20 minutes without the whistle.
7) Peel off the leaf and serve with ghee.

Variation
In case you are unable to source fresh turmeric leaves use banana leaves.

Recipe No 32: Chana Dal Payasam
(Serves 2)

Ingredients
- 1 cup chana dal
- 3 cups of water
- 2 tbsp of ghee
- 1 cup of coconut milk
- ¼ cup of finely chopped coconut
- 1 cup of jaggery
- ½ tsp green cardamom (elaichi) powder
- ½ cup of finely chopped dry fruits (almonds, cashew and raisins)

Preparation
1) In a pressure cooker add the chana dal and 3 cups of water and pressure cook the same.
2) Once cooked, add the chopped coconut pieces and jaggery to the chana dal and boil till the jaggery dissolves.
3) Add the coconut milk and boil for 5 minutes.
4) Add ghee and the cardamom powder and garnish with the dry fruits.

Variation
Chana dal can be replaced with Moong dal.

A Mother's Dream

We have also been introduced to individuals who were more than extended family. My Ajji had cut ties with her immediate family, because she experienced a lot of exclusion from them. She always maintained that family is not about blood, it's about who is willing to hold your hand when you need it the most. With time new relations were formed. All my Maamas, Aunts and my Mother's friends became an integral part of the family. Some of them would address her as 'Amma' (meaning Mother) like she would be addressed by her own kids. Later on, their spouses and kids were also integrated with the family. I would like to mention here two such relations – one was my Maama's flat mate – Seshu Maama and the other my Mother's nursing friend whom we all addressed as Bandi Maushi. Seshu Maama was posted in North Canara and on most vacations, we would visit him for days together. The same was with Bandi Maushi and her husband Joe uncle. Joe uncle to this day remembers the fish curry preparation of my Ajji and claims that to be a preparation that no one can match up to. Bandi maushi also very fondly recalls her interaction with my Ajji and the fact that they have nurtured the relationship and bond for close to seven decades now.

Both my Maama and Maami fondly recall that she played the role of being the custodian of the family, especially with them struggling in the initial period of their family life with young children and careers to manage. My Maama recalls that he would hand over his salary to her every month along with details of other investments and securities. And she would aptly keep all accounts ready for easy access and understanding for my Maama to manage the actual show. My Maama recalls with amusement that she had a 'Safe vault" in which she would keep all the money and gold. And she was very protective of it. The keys to the vault were in her sole custody which she would not hand over to anyone. I have memories of seeing the key anchored in a chain around her neck. It was her most precious possession. If my Maama or Maami needed anything from it, she would be the one to open the vault and pull out the money or gold and hand it over to them. Nobody in the household had access to it. So much so, that all the grandchildren would wonder and be very inquisitive to know what was the 'treasure' that was stored in it and we would make plans to smuggle the key to explore this treasure. But alas! The plan was never a success. Because she was the custodian of the treasure generated by her son and she was determined to guard it with her life.

It seems a few days before her death, some six to seven days before Good Friday of 1988, to be precise, my Ajji called my Maami and handed over the vault keys to her and said, "starting from now you are the custodian of everything that belongs to my son."

I guess she had some premonition of her departing and thus wanted to pass on the mantle to my Maami, which she continues to anchor till date. My Ajji passed away on Good Friday of year 1988, 1st April 1988. It has been thirty-two years since, but to this day all her children and their families gather to remember her on her death anniversary. On this day, food of her liking is prepared which we all relish and the day is spent in remembering and cherishing her memories.

I would like to end this narration on the note, that life throws its challenges in very phase of life. It is our attitude towards it that determines the outcome. What I have learnt from my Ajji, is to have a dream for yourself and work towards it without any second thoughts. This combined with faith in yourself and God will make things to start unfolding as per your dreams. It is so rightly said that when one has a deep desire for things in life, the entire universe will conspire to make it a reality. What is important is to believe in your dreams!

"Keep your heart open to dreams. For as long as there's a dream, there is hope, and as long as there is hope, there is joy in living."
- Unknown Author

List of Recipes	Page No
1. Aambil	28
2. Mumri (Thalipeeth)	30
3. Poha (Beaten rice)	32
4. Sweet Poha - Traditionally called Hashaal	33
5. Idli Chura	34
6. Red pumpkin Dhodak (dhokla)	35
7. Fish Curry	43-44
8. Mackerel Triphal Curry	46-47
9. Udid Methi Mackerel	48-49
10. Aamshetikshe	50-51
11. Hinga Tamli	55
12. Fish Fry	56-57
13. Jeera Meera Egg Curry	58-59
14. Bhendi Kadi (Lady Finger)	60-61
15. Raw Mango Ghashi (curry)	62-63
16. Ambya Sasum (Mango Raita)	63
17. Mande	65-67
18. Garlic Chutney	84
19. Cucumber Chutney	85
20. Sweet and sour Mango chutney	86
21. Dry prawn chutney	87
22. Karela (Bitter gourd) Chutney	88
23. Karela Ghashi	89-90
24. Karela Amshetikshe	91-92
25. Karela vegetable	93
26. Kholumbo	99-100
27. Tisre Masala (clams)	103-104
28. Mutton Curry	105-107
29. Layered Mutton Biryani	108-111
30. Coconut rice	112
31. Patole (steamed rice rolls)	113-114
32. Chana dal payasam	115

Some general cooking tips

The Karwar cuisine is extremely delectable and has at its core three main ingredients: fish, rice and fresh coconut. The spices that add to the flavor are dry red chili, cumin seeds, coriander seeds, fenugreek, triphal, tamarind and kokum petals. By and large pure coconut oil is preferred in cooking fish as it adds to its aroma and taste.

Fish

The fish used is sea fish. River fish is not consumed much in this region. Hence, if one uses river fish there will be noticeable difference in the taste of the food being cooked. Fish that is majorly available in this region is: Mackerel, Sliver fish (Motiyal or Belongi) Promfret, Surmai (Seer fish / King fish), Moori (baby shark), Black Promfret, Tarle (Sardines) and Karli (Silver bar fish), Shatka, Nogli (lady fish), Ravas and some other variety. In terms of shellfish, it is Prawns, Clams & Oysters (Tisre, Khubbe and Kalwa) and Crabs.

Some sea fish like Mackerel, Moori (baby shark), Black Promfret, Tarle (sardines) and Karli (Silver Bar fish) tend to have a strong unpleasant fishy smell. To tame down this smell apply some turmeric powder, salt and lime juice to the cleaned cut pieces of fish and let it rest for 10 to 15 minutes. Then rinse thoroughly with water and process as the recipe guidelines.

Tarle (sardines) and Karli are very tasty. However, one drawback is that it has many bones. Karli especially has to be cut in a particular manner. The cutting technique used is the slant cuts.

Cooking time for fish is about 5 to 10 minutes. Please note once cooked the fish becomes very tender and hence it should be handled delicately while stirring or frying to ensure it does not break.

It is also recommended that fish curry preparations should be cooked at least two to three hours before the meal time. The longer the rest time once the dish is cooked the better it tastes.

Spices
Dry red chili the Byadgi variety is generally used. This is less spicy and gives a nice color. If you are using any another variety of chili, please use your judgment in-terms of the proportions to ensure an edible spicy level.

Triphal is also a very commonly used spice in the Karwar cuisine. It is very pungent. And hence the technique is to slightly crush it and add to the preparation.

Oil
Most of the fish cooking is recommend in pure coconut oil. It's just that one has to develop a taste to it. Mark my word, once you develop the taste of fish cooked in pure coconut oil you will not ever want to try the Karwar fish curry cooked in any other cooking oil.

Kokum and Tamarind
These are used to get the tangy flavor.

Printed in Dunstable, United Kingdom